W9-CLC-043

Person to Person

PERSON TO PERSON

A Handbook for
PASTORAL COUNSELING

by
JAMES A. VANDERPOOL, Ph.D.

DOUBLEDAY & COMPANY, INC.
Garden City, New York
1977

253.5
VA p

Library of Congress Cataloging in Publication Data

Vanderpool, James A
Person to person.

Bibliography
1. Pastoral counseling—Handbooks, manuals, etc.
I. Title.
BV4012.2.V28   253.5
ISBN: 0-385-12518-6
Library of Congress Catalog Card Number 76-20837

CONTENTS

Preface

There are many good books on pastoral counseling. One may ask why there should be another one. I wrote it because I thought it was needed and I was asked to do so by many whom I respect and love.

It has been said to me many times: "There are many books which you recommend when you lecture on pastoral theology and pastoral counseling, but I can't buy a library and carry it with me into a parish or a mission field. Can't you recommend one book that can serve as a handbook for me in my work as a pastoral counselor?" In every case, I have had to say no.

I was finally challenged to write this book by a woman who served as a pastoral counselor in a remote mission field. She and her associates asked for a book that did three things: (1) defined and explained the unique role of a pastor as a counselor; (2) a book which was not expected to deal in depth in any particular area but would assist the pastoral counselor in dealing with all stages and phases of human life; and (3) would help the pastor develop techniques and means to fulfill the special role of counselor. The woman tape-recorded a series of lectures I gave; she sent them to me with an urgent request to use them as a basis for a book. This I did.

The author's background is unique and varied. My father and four uncles were Methodist ministers. I became an Anglican priest and then a Roman Catholic priest. For twenty years I served as pastor of a large parish in the diocese of Rockford, Illinois. During that time I served on the Cana and Pre-Cana teams as a member of the diocesan Family Life Bureau. After obtaining a doctor's degree in clinical psychology, I was permitted to accept a position as the clinical director of the world's largest alcoholic treatment center, in the District of Columbia government. While in this position, I joined the staff as part-time professor of pastoral theology at the Washington Theological Coalition and Consortium. These schools are attended by both Protestant and Catholic students of both sexes. In addition, I am a regular lecturer and conductor of seminars in pastoral theology and pastoral counseling, including those held for missionaries from all over the world by the United States Catholic Mission Conference.

This book is offered, therefore, as a handbook to help a pastor in the many areas of pastoral counseling and to encourage and help the counselor to be a competent one and to help the pastor understand the specific privilege and duty that he or she alone can perform.

Although written by a Catholic priest, who is also a diplomate in clinical psychology,' this handbook is written to assist any and all, male or female, Protestant, Catholic, Jewish, or other, pastoral counselor to perform more effectively as a pastoral counselor.

The author is grateful to all those, both living and dead, who during his fifty-eight years have served as his teachers, guides, educators, friends, parishioners, penitents, clients, or critics. The illustrations in this handbook are based on actual cases; the names, places, circumstances, etc., however, have been changed to insure confidentiality of any privileged information and have been altered when necessary to make a specific point.

As the author, I am indebted to many people who have made this work possible. I am grateful to a Roman Catholic sister, who wishes to remain anonymous, who sent me the tapes of my lectures. And to Rosalie V. Smoot who helped transcribe some of the first draft of this book from the tapes.

I am indebted and grateful to my wonderful friend and secretary, Mrs. George (Ruby) Heflin, who faithfully transcribed and typed many revisions and the final copy for this manuscript.

One person stands out as one the author cannot thank adequately. He is Dr. Ray B. Smith, Ph.D., my intimate friend and professional associate who serves as Chief of Research and Training in my department at the Rehabilitation Center for Alcoholics and Veteran's

Home for the District of Columbia government at Occoquan, Virginia. Dr. Smith not only helped me in my attempts to overcome stylized and ambiguous writing but also contributed ideas, illustrations, and even concepts for this handbook. For this reason—since he did not feel it was proper to give him credit as a coauthor—he is acknowledged and thanked for serving as a collaborator for this work.

Finally, my thanks to all those countless human beings who have trusted me and have involved themselves as clients with me as their counselor and have permitted me to contribute to their moral and spiritual value systems, and, it is hoped to their personal fulfillment and actualization.

J.A.V.

Person to Person

I

Pastoral Counseling

1

PASTORAL THEOLOGY AND PASTORAL COUNSELING

Introduction

There are many ways in which the pastor makes the teachings of the Christian faith relevant for people. The ordained priest or minister does so through preaching and the pulpit; he does so through the Liturgy, in the confessional, while on sick calls, in the school, in the home, and in the rectory or parsonage. All of these are important means for teaching the Christian truths; however, one of the most important means for applying these truths to individuals in specific situations is through pastoral counseling. To be an effective pastor today, one needs to be a good pastoral counselor. The chief purpose of this handbook is to assist the pastor in being an efficient and effective pastoral counselor.

Many pastors are reluctant to do counseling. Why? Because the risk one must take can be frightening and distasteful. When dogma is presented to the people, the minister has scripture, church declarations, creeds, and other dogmatic decrees to fall back on for support; when he proclaims moral principles to the people, he has scripture, the Ten Commandments, the two great commandments, and church decrees to support and defend him. When, however, he accepts the role of a pastoral counselor, he has no external supports or instruments to use. The pastor, as counselor, has only his own person and his own personality to be his tools or instruments for dispensing pastoral care. It is easy for the minister or priest to declare Christian teachings when he is safely isolated from the people in the pulpit; it is another thing to be associated in the intimate relationship on a one-to-one basis which counseling often necessitates. This relationship creates the risk. He must risk being ridiculed, embarrassed, laughed at, rejected, seduced, loved, hated, and misunderstood. He must risk being human; he may get personally and emotionally involved—so much so at times that he must disqualify himself; he will make mistakes at times; he will feel pain and hurt himself in some instances; he may be subject on occasion to bodily harm and danger. It is understandable, although regrettable, that many ministers and priests are reluctant to do pastoral counseling. It is too dangerous; it involves too great a risk—it involves being human—in becoming incarnate. Our Lord, the Model Pastor, did not hesitate to be a counselor; he accepted the risk and dangers even though, ultimately, it meant His death on the cross.

In the past ten or fifteen years the need for pastors who are willing to go out to the people has increased. In the past it was often true that many of the clergy were content to stay in their ivory towers—the rectories or parsonages—and "dispense" pastoral care to the people who had to come to them. Rarely did they go out to the people—occasionally to attend a wedding celebration or to make a sick call. Most of the time they remained aloof and unapproachable. Today such a ministry is ineffective. Today the pastor must leave the security and safety of the rectory or parsonage and give pastoral care to people where they live; he must make the truths of the Christian faith relevant to each individual in his day-to-day life situation regardless of the personal risk this involves. In imitation of Our Blessed Lord, whom he is supposed to emulate, the pastor must be willing to involve himself with people and their unique problems. He must go, as the good pastor the late Pope John did, into the prison and care for the prisoner; he must sit down with the poor, as the great saints of old did, and help them with their problems; he must give loving care to individuals whose appearance may be repulsive because of the ravages of sickness and disease, as Father Damien did for the lepers; he must be willing to sit down with the morally degenerate, no matter how heinous his offense may have been, and love, genuinely, the person.

Pastoral Theology

Pastoral theology is concerned with the application of moral and dogmatic theology to a unique person in a specific situation and at a given point in time. It seeks to apply the truths of the Christian faith to the life and needs of a black man in an African village, to an American Indian on a southwestern reservation, to a bright young lawyer in a large city, to a mentally retarded child in an institution, to a seminarian beginning his studies, to a Hindu in India, to a mother after giving birth to a baby, to a dying elderly man—to any and all individuals at all times and places. It is an existential theology in that it seeks to make moral theology, dogma, the Church, scripture, creeds, codes, and cults relevant to each person here and now.

Pastoral theology is difficult because, unlike moral and dogmatic theology, there are no absolutes. There are no blacks or whites. The truths of the Christian faith apply in a different way for each person in every situation. A young drug addict steals in order to get money to buy drugs; an unemployed father steals in order to buy bread for his starving children; a rich young boy who suffers from kleptomania steals for no rational or apparent reason. All three have stolen but the application of Christian moral principles must be different in each case.

Pastoral theology requires that the pastor recognize the difference between objective truth—what a thing really is—and subjective truth—what one thinks a thing is. Objectively, an airplane may be flying high in the sky; someone mistakenly thinks it is a bird. Subjective truth for that individual is that the object in the sky is a bird.

In order to apply the truths of the Christian faith, a pastor, in his role as counselor, must understand and accept the implications of not only true and erroneous but also certain and doubtful conscience as well. By definition, "conscience" is the intellect judging the goodness or badness of an act to be performed. A father promises to reward his son with a dollar if he studies hard and improves his grades in school. The boy brings home his next report card and the father is pleased to see higher grades and feels obliged to reward the child. The father assumes that the boy has improved his grades by studying harder than before. In reality the objective truth was that the boy had a new teacher who graded higher than his former teacher; he has not studied any harder than he had before. However, his father thinks he has studied harder—this is subjective truth for the father. The father then forms a certain conscience—but an erroneous conscience—that the boy has studied harder. He feels he is obliged to follow this certain conscience and reward the boy with the dollar he promised, otherwise he would be guilty of violating his conscience. The father must follow his certain conscience even when it is erroneous; if he does not he is morally culpable.

The pastor must accept this moral principle in dealing with individuals and acts performed by individuals. Every individual is bound, morally, to follow a certain conscience—if there has been a genuine effort to form a true conscience—even if it is erroneous. This moral principle has far reaching implications particularly for the pastor in counseling. This is why pastoral counseling must, by theological definition, be existential.

A second important point is that, above all, pastoral theology is concerned with the person; the person's behavior, feelings, attitudes, or thoughts are secondary. A pastor is concerned about the boy who masturbates and is concerned about the guilt feelings the boy has because of his masturbation. In his role as pastoral counselor he is not concerned, primarily, about the masturbation or his own moral theology concerning masturbation. Everything is secondary to his concern for the boy and the pain he feels because of his behavior. It is essential that in his role of pastoral counselor, the minister, the priest, the brother, the sister, or the layman must be willing and able to distinguish between a person who must be accepted, loved, and understood and the person's behavior, of which he need not approve. A man comes to the pastor because he feels guilty about his sexual promiscuity and his unfaithfulness to his wife and family. Although the pastor does not approve of his behavior, he loves the person and seeks to help him in any way he can.

In his role as pastor, then, the pastor is not concerned primarily about what is right or wrong objectively. In each case, he is concerned about a person who is suffering—perhaps because of feelings of guilt; he seeks to heal the person regardless of the person's problem or behavior. He strives to imitate the Model Pastor, Our Blessed Lord, who cared about people as such, regardless of their problems, their attitudes, or their behavior. Our Lord sat down at a well one day and counseled an adulterous woman. He did not approve of her adultery but He showed great compassion and love for the woman herself. Even at the cross, He showed great love for a former prostitute, Mary Magdalen, by permitting her to be the only person present except His Blessed Mother and the disciple whom He loved, St. John.

The Pastor

The word "pastor" comes from the Latin and means "a shepherd"; it is related to the Latin *pascere* which in English means "to feed." Hence, a pastor is one who, like a shepherd, cares for and watches over his sheep and helps find nourishment for them. In modern times the term is used, ordinarily, to indicate an ordained clergyman who is in charge of a congregation. In this book it will be used in a more generic and less specific way. On the one hand, it will be used to describe and discuss the role of the ordained clergyman—priest or minister—in his role as a pastoral counselor alone, but in no other way—not as one in charge of a church, not as one functioning as a preacher, not as an administrator of sacraments; only as one in his role as a pastor who counsels people. On the other hand, the term "pastor" will not be limited to a specific ministry of ordained clergymen. When "pastor" is used it is to be understood that the function of pastor may be exercised by brothers, sisters, and laymen. The term pastor intends to include, henceforth, anyone who counsels individuals regarding problems which involve guilt feelings or an individual's moral, theological, and certain personal values.

Pastoral Counseling

Counseling is not to be confused with education, guidance, or psychotherapy. Education implies that one is lead by an expert—the teacher—to the knowledge or to an increased knowledge of a subject.

The geography teacher in the school educates the students when he leads the students to a knowledge about the world about him. Often the minister or priest is an educator when he teaches his congregation the truths of the Christian faith from the pulpit, in the classroom, and through study groups.

Guidance is used in a more restricted sense than education. A guide not only gives information about a subject but also seeks to lead the one being guided to expertise in the subject or seeks to help the individual find ways and means to become proficient and an expert in a field. The guide who leads a person up the mountain and trains him to be a mountain climber is giving guidance. The counselor in a high school who assists a student to appraise his interest and abilities and then helps him find ways and means to learn the trade or skill is giving guidance. The ordained minister or priest is involved often in guidance—in the confessional, in marriage and premarital conferences, in classes he may teach in a seminary, and in many other ways.

Counseling differs from psychotherapy in two important ways. Counselors should deal with the normal problems of normal and disturbed people and should try to help the client find more adaptive ways to handle his problems than he may have in the past in terms of his own value system. The psychotherapist is the only one who should deal with the abnormal problems of both normal and disturbed people. In many cases this will, possibly, necessitate an attempt by the therapist to change the personality structure of the individual.

A teenager comes to a counselor because he feels tense and awkward because of his rapid growth. Maladaptively, he releases the anxiety that this tension causes by hostile and aggressive behavior toward his brothers and sisters at home. To feel tense and awkward during adolescence is a normal problem; it is a proper problem for a counselor to handle. However, the teenager is handling the problem and its attendant anxiety in a maladaptive way—he is hostile and aggressive at home. No attempt is made by the counselor to change the personality structure of the boy; he can, however, help the boy find more adaptive ways for handling the tension. He can suggest several alternative, adaptive ways to handle the problem and the anxiety. He may suggest that the young man take a more active part in sports; he may suggest that he find someone who can help him use corrective exercises to overcome the awkwardness; he may suggest any number of behavioral alternatives to the maladaptive hostile and aggressive behavior in his home.

Again, a man with an abnormal emotional problem comes to the counselor. He is estranged from his wife and family and now spends his lonely hours drinking excessively in a bar. The counselor cannot —and should not—try to handle the abnormal problem which is the cause of the emotional disturbance. He can help this same man with the normal problem which has arisen because he is alienated from his family and help him find adaptive ways to handle his loneliness other than excessive drinking.

Clearly, then, the role of counselor does not include handling the abnormal problems of either normal or disturbed people. He needs, however, to recognize such problems and refer the client to a psycho-therapist. For example, a hysterical woman comes to the counselor and complains incessantly about her real or imaginary aches and pains which have no apparent cause. He does not try to handle her deep-seated psychological problems but refers her to a doctor or a psychotherapist.

Another aspect of counseling is "crisis intervention," when a special or unusual problem arises in the life of an otherwise normal individual which the individual handles in a maladaptive or unhealthy way. The counselor intervenes and helps the person find alternative adaptive ways to handle the problem at the moment and the anxiety it produces.

For example, a man's wife is killed in an automobile accident. He begins to go to a bar each night and tries to drown his sorrow in alcohol and turns against his religion. "How could anyone love and worship a God who would let my wife's life be snuffed out in her prime when she was such a perfect wife and mother?" he asks the pastor. The pastor lets him know that he understands the pain and does not understand why her death should have occurred. He does not try to play God and give reasons for her death. Instead, he points out to the man that he is destroying himself by his maladaptive way of handling his normal and understandable grief. This behavior would be the last thing his wife would want. She would want him to double his efforts to sustain the family without her and preserve the moral and religious value system she—and he—had developed for the family.

In brief, a counselor seeks to help a client find a more rewarding way to think, feel, or behave. He is not expected to treat abnormal problems of people; he is not expected to try to change the personality structure of an individual. He is expected to assist people to achieve their goals of everyday living adaptively.

The pastor must do what counselors in general do. He must learn to recognize and distinguish between normal and abnormal problems of people; he must be able to help those who come to him find ways of handling their problems either by referral or by suggesting more adaptive ways to handle them than they have in the past.

Pastoral counseling, however, has a certain uniqueness. It includes a specific type of counseling which deals with problems of guilt and with concerns regarding values as they exist for each individual, particularly their moral, religious and spiritual values.

When a pastor counsels a student in high school regarding his future vocation, he is being simply a vocational counselor; when he counsels young couples regarding marriage, he is functioning as any marriage counselor; when, however, he is counseling individuals about their feelings of guilt or about their values and value systems he is serving in the unique role as a pastoral counselor. "Guilt" and "values"—these are the two areas in which the pastoral counselor must be expert and knowledgeable. He must be ready and prepared to handle the guilt feelings of a man who sexually desires a woman and wishes he did not; he must be prepared to handle the guilt feelings of a woman who has stolen goods from a department store; he must be prepared to help an individual develop his or her own moral, spiritual, and personal value system and then help the person to find realistic ways to achieve his objectives and goals within that value system.

Human Personality and Human Behavior

To be an effective pastoral counselor, one needs to know certain basic facts regarding human personality and human behavior. It is beyond the scope of this book to treat these in detail; a brief summary of certain facts will be helpful to the counselor.

Christians recognize that man is made of body and soul; the soul is the vital principle for the animal body. From a biological and psychological point of view, however, there are three main determinants of personality, namely, heredity, the environment, and the self, or ego, which develops from and is determined by heredity and environment. A boy is short because both his parents are short; a girl is dark-skinned because her parents are dark-skinned. These illustrate genetic heredity which affects the later personality development.

Perhaps affecting personality development even more is the environmental inheritance and influence. For example, a young man is successful in business because he is not only intelligent but also was able, financially, to attend one of the best universities and has a mature personality structure; a young woman is a good homemaker because she was brought up in a home environment where her mother made an art of making a home and she feels competent and secure in this role; a boy is brought up in a slum ghetto and turns to crime as an outlet for his aggressive, hostile personality; a little girl does not develop physically or mentally as she should because she has experienced near starvation, war, and hunger, and as an adult she is shy, fearful, and retiring—all these and similar environmental factors are determinants of human personality.

Finally, the self, or ego, and its characteristics is a critical determinant of human personality. Under the direction and loving care of mature parents, a child feels secure and develops a strong ego, which later in life is able to withstand the pressures and the anxiety that life's stresses and strains produce; a man thirty years of age becomes neurotic because he feels inadequate and has little ego strength—he is dependent and immature. His parents overprotected him and did not serve as adequate models as he developed emotionally. To repeat, heredity and environment as they interact determine the ego structure and determine the personality structure and development of the personality of each individual.

There are certain motivations or basic strivings which determine the direction of human behavior and activate the person to action. Some of these are biological; others are psychological.

A. H. Maslow, Ph.D., suggests that there is a hierarchy of needs

which prompts behavior and determines its direction: physiological
needs such as hunger, thirst, and all things needed to sustain life;
the need for safety and security—to have a home, to belong to a community, to belong to a country; the need to love and be loved—the
need to share maturely one's real self with the real self of another;
the need for self-esteem and the esteem of others because of one's
own personal and unique worth; and finally the need for self-actualization—the need to create and realize one's creative potentiali-
ties.

Christians, and others, recognize certain other needs which moti-
vate human behavior and activate the human to action; chief among
these are human spiritual needs.

James Coleman suggests that there are six basic psychological
needs: (1) the need for order and meaning for one's life; (2) the
need to feel adequate and competent; (3) the need for security; (4)
the need for social approval, a sense of belongingness and status; (5)
the need for self-esteem and feelings of personal worth; and (6) the
need for love and relatedness.

The human organism like all organisms tends to homeostatic
equilibrium—that is, to a state of balance, rest, and stability. When
this homeostatic equilibrium is disturbed because some biological,
psychological, or spiritual need is not satisfied, the human organism
mobilizes energy for needed action to restore homeostatic equilibrium. When a person is hungry, the need for food disturbs physiological equilibrium; the human organism is mobilized to action and
the person seeks food to restore the homeostatic equilibrium.

Similarly, emotions and other psychological drives and needs
which disturb the homeostatic equilibrium in man mobilize the
human to action—emotions such as fear, anger, attraction, repulsion,
liking, or disliking can disturb this equilibrium. Emotional pain and
pleasure; stress and strain; tension and anxiety; all are important as
motivators and energizers to human action. Most important to the
pastor is the homeostatic disturbance to the individual who has not
developed an adequate personal, moral, and theological system of
values and the disturbances caused by guilt that has not been alleviated because of unresolved spiritual needs.

Anxiety

Anxiety is one of the first signs of any disturbance to homeostatic equilibrium. Psychologically speaking, anxiety acts like steam in a teakettle in a human organism. If it is not released, it disturbs the homeostatic equilibrium of the human organism further and may cause serious damage to the self or ego even to the point of mental illness.

Three types of stresses and strains which produce anxiety in the human organism are frustrations, conflicts, and pressures.

1. *Frustration* occurs when one wants something and cannot have it, that is, cannot find a way to achieve a goal. A man wants to be a doctor but he has no doctor's degree—he is frustrated in his desire to be a doctor. A woman wants to be an actress but she has set an unrealistic goal for herself because she cannot act and no one will hire her—she is frustrated.

2. *Conflict* arises in the presence of two or more contradictory goals which by definition cannot both be achieved. A man wants to be a Roman Catholic priest which means he must remain celibate; he wants, also, to be married. This is a serious conflict and remains one for many such priests throughout their lives.

3. *Pressures* are a third type of stresses and strains which may cause anxiety. These arise when one encounters difficulty in achieving a goal. These pressures may be external or internal. A girl's mother forces her to work hard in an attempt to make the girl a TV star. The mother was frustrated in her desire to be a star and acts out her frustration by attempting to force her daughter to be the star she could not be; the child cannot act any better than her mother. Further, the child has not accepted acting as a goal. Her goal is to avoid this enforced role of acting. As the mother's frustration increases, the child becomes anxious as a result of this external parental pressure. In addition, the girl's internal pressure increases because her own avoidance goal is not being met.

Or, a man sets for himself an unrealistic goal of becoming a great

athlete and pushes himself to the limit to accomplish the goal.
When he fails to reach his goal, he continues to push himself. Anxiety will be built up increasingly in the man because the internal
pressure to succeed is beyond his ability to reach that goal.

To restate, anxiety is a psychological pressure which must be
released or it can damage the self seriously or even cause disintegration and destruction of the ego. To release and dissipate anxiety
the human organism adopts and uses various coping mechanisms.
These are classified as adaptive, semiadaptive, and maladaptive
mechanisms.

Coping Mechanisms

1. *Adaptive mechanisms.* When one is able to find and use an adaptive—or healthy—mechanism to alleviate anxiety, not only is the anxiety handled but also the ego is strengthened and the self-concept of
the individual improved. Among the principle types of adaptive
mechanisms are attack, withdrawal, and compromise mechanisms.

a. To attack a problem means that one faces a problem realistically and solves it. For example, someone wants to be a painter but
he does not have any training. He goes to art school—he attacks the
problem realistically—he studies and obtains the desired skill.

b. Withdrawal is the adaptive mechanism used when one realizes that a goal cannot be reached or a problem solved by attacking
it. A man dislikes another man. He knows, however, that if he
confronts the man he will, personally, get hurt. One adaptive way
to handle the situation and the anxiety it causes is to withdraw—to
get away from the person who is causing the problem.

c. Compromise is a third adaptive means of handling anxiety
caused by stress and strain. Compromise as used in psychology is not
a moral concept meaning that one compromises his moral principles;
it is a term to describe adaptive mechanisms of this particular type.
Compromise implies that one recognizes that he cannot have something he wants immediately because of some obstacle and he is
willing to wait to achieve the goal until the obstacle is removed or
even substitute a different goal.

To illustrate, earlier it was suggested that the anxiety caused by being frustrated in becoming an artist could be solved by attacking the problem—by the individual going to school and obtaining the requisite skills. Suppose, however, that the individual cannot enter art school immediately because he does not have the money for the tuition. Using the mechanism of compromise, he alleviates his anxiety by holding on to his goal but postponing entering art school until later. To remove the obstacle to his goal, he goes to work in a factory until he can obtain enough money for art school.

2. *Semiadaptive mechanisms.* There are many semiadaptive mechanisms, none of which handles all of the anxiety. Two are particularly important for the pastoral counselor to understand. These are the mechanisms known as "sublimation" and "reaction formation."

a. Sublimation is a semiadaptive mechanism which may be used by a person when he cannot—or is not permitted to—attain a goal. For example, a young man studying for the Roman Catholic priesthood is normal and has the same sexual desires as other men. He is told that he may not satisfy his sexual desires or urges in any overt or covert way. He must then at all times "sublimate" these desires. How does he sublimate? He is told to keep very busy, for example, by participating in athletics, by being with a large group of people rather than being alone and to avoid being alone with only one or two other persons and turn his mind to other things when he feels these forbidden urges.

Experience has shown that a great deal of exercise—particularly, that undertaken by one who loathes any form of strenuous physical activity—will render all animal drives less intense. Again, being with many people or keeping very busy may distract the seminarian's attention from sex. But all of these attempts to cope with anxiety by sublimation never completely alleviate the tension and anxiety which the frustration of these desires produces. At best, sublimation activities may lessen or weaken a focused sex urge; they never completely and adaptively get rid of the urges and their attendant anxiety.

b. Another semiadaptive defense mechanism is reaction formation, behaving opposite to the way one basically feels. In a survey made of priests and seminarians in a large midwestern Roman Catholic archdiocese, this mechanism, along with sublimation was found to be the one most commonly used by them.

A man dislikes another man and feels very hostile toward him. He knows, however, that he dare not show his dislike and start a fight because the other man is bigger and stronger than he is. Earlier it was indicated that one adaptive mechanism to use to alleviate the tension and anxiety this situation might produce was withdrawal. In some cases one cannot leave a situation, that is, he cannot withdraw. If he cannot find an adaptive way to handle the anxiety this situation causes, "reaction formation" is a semiadaptive mechanism that may be helpful in that some of the tension and anxiety are alleviated and the intensity of the emotional stress decreased. In this case the man's reaction formation is shown in a deliberate attempt to cultivate friendship in a man he dislikes intensely.

Another common example of reaction formation is used by a girl in a junior high school who pretends to dislike another girl—making deprecating comments at every opportunity—for whom, indeed, she feels a very strong emotional attachment.

For forty years a minister's wife was able to keep her husband from being fired by using this type of reaction-formation as a defense mechanism. This woman was never allowed to decorate the parsonage in which the family lived or determine the furniture to be placed in the parsonage. Instead, a group of women in the church, who, seemingly, had nothing else to do except mind other people's business, served as a committee to decorate and furnish the parsonage. Invariably, this committee would bring all the junk they did not want in their own homes and put it in the parsonage. This caused not only frustration for the minister's wife but also caused the minister and the rest of the family to become very hostile toward the women. Many times the minister wanted to tell this committee what he thought of them, but his wife would plead with him not to do so because he would be fired. After a near explosion by the minister, the wife, who basically liked the members of the committee no better than her husband did, would say, "Sister Jones means well; she really has a good heart; she is really a devout and loyal member of the congregation," etc. In no way did this use of reaction formation completely alleviate the tension, the hostility, and the accompanying anxiety. It did, however, work sufficiently well to prevent many disasterous blow-ups between the minister and the women in his congregation.

3. *Maladaptive mechanisms.* The third class of major defense mechanisms are called "maladaptive" or "unhealthy" mechanisms. These are maladaptive not only because they do not get rid of the anxiety, but also because they frequently increase anxiety. Two of the frequently used maladaptive defense mechanisms are called "suppression" and "repression."

a. In suppression, one is aware of a disturbing situation or stress and attempts to keep it out of his conscious mind as much as possible because it is most stressful only when he is thinking about it.

For example, a married man is surprised to find himself feeling strongly attracted to the new bachelor who has just moved in next door. This creates conflict, stress, and anxiety in him. In his effort to suppress these unwanted feelings, he deliberately avoids his new neighbor and makes every effort not to think about him. Only when the presence of the neighbor intrudes itself into his conscious mind does he feel anxiety, but the underlying anxiety, because of the original feeling, must remain until he finds a more adaptive way to handle it.

b. Repression involves the inability to face a situation or stress head on because the existence of the stressor has been denied at the conscious level.

To illustrate, a woman was a patient in a midwestern mental institution. All day long she would wring her hands without stopping. It was recognized that this wringing of her hands was, symbolically, a hand-washing ritual. The hand-washing ritual, in turn, was a symbolic attempt to wash away guilt which she had repressed. The clinician placed her in therapy. It turned out that the woman was a very pious and religious woman, who had had an affair with a boy when she was twelve or thirteen. She could not face the guilt she felt for this act and felt, in herself, there could be no forgiveness for her for such behavior. After the affair she kept saying to herself: "I didn't do it; I didn't do it; I really didn't do it." And later added to her lie: "I really didn't do it; I only dreamed I did it." As the years went on, the memory of the whole affair left her conscious mind so that for her it did not exist. This is "repression."

What had happened in reality? She had never handled the anxiety; it had been pushed down inside of her—but the anxiety was still there and evidenced itself in her ritualistic hand washing. With the help of the clinician, she faced the truth; she faced her guilt feelings and felt sure that she could be forgiven. She no longer used her maladaptive mechanisms and ceased her hand wringing and other neurotic behavior. In time it was possible for her to leave the mental hospital and to return to normal life.

The pastoral counselor is not expected to handle deep-seated problems of repression but adds his unique role in handling the guilt once the repression has been resolved by the clinician.

Mental Health

Strictly speaking, there is no such thing as a person with perfect mental health; there is no human who cannot, potentially, become mentally ill. Mental health depends on many factors, but two are most important, namely, ego strength and the amount of stress and strain impinging on the ego. There is a limit to the stress and strain that any human can endure. This was tragically demonstrated by the mental breakdowns and illnesses which occurred to otherwise mentally healthy individuals when subjected to the stress and strain of combat in war. As the body has its limits, so does the mind; even the strongest can undergo enough stress and strain to cause mental illness. A definition of "normal" mental health can, therefore, be only an operational one. For the purposes of the pastoral counselor, the term "normal" will be used to describe a person who has made a relatively good adjustment to himself, to his environment, to others, to society, and—for the Christian and other religious—to God and His Universe.

To rephrase, one of the chief goals of counseling is to assist a client to achieve or improve his mental health by assisting him to improve his adjustment in relationship to himself and others. Or, as C. H. Patterson, Ph.D., says, the ultimate goals of counseling are to assist the client to a responsible independence in the external forum and to self-realization in the internal forum.

The pastoral counselor has the same goals and objectives as all other counselors. In a special way, he seeks to help a client find adaptive ways to handle feelings of guilt and to handle problems involving the client's value system, particularly those involving his moral and religious values.

Guilt

Guilt is the painful feeling of self-reproach resulting from a belief that one has felt, said, thought, or done something wrong or immoral or has failed to do something which he feels, morally, he should have done. Feelings, thoughts, words, deeds, and omissions—these five are the chief bases for guilt feelings. One may feel guilty because he performs some forbidden act of aggression; he may, however, feel guilty because he simply feels attracted to another person. One may feel guilty because he cursed his neighbor; he may feel guilty because of what he thinks about that neighbor. Again, one may feel guilty for omitting doing something he thinks he should do —a man fails to go to church on Sunday when he feels he is morally obliged to do so; a woman feels guilty because she played cards all afternoon and failed to prepare the dinner for her family that she thinks she should.

It is a special duty of the pastor as counselor to assist clients to find ways to handle guilt feelings regardless of their source or cause. To do this he must know and teach his clients the difference between two types of guilt—one is called "emotional" or "irrational" guilt and the other is called "rational" or "moral" guilt.

1. *Irrational guilt.* Man, along with all other animals, has animal emotions. These emotions are irrational and arise spontaneously; they are not under the control of the intellect. One's likes or dislikes are generally irrational feelings; one's attractions for or revulsions to things are also the result of irrational emotions. One man is attracted to blond women; another man is repelled by tall women. One woman is afraid of heights; another woman is terrified of snakes. These are all irrational animal emotions.

Because emotions are irrational and animal, they should not ever be the cause of feelings of guilt in individuals, but they sometimes are. Such guilt, when it occurs, is emotional or irrational guilt. A man sexually desires a beautiful woman and feels guilty for such a desire; the guilt feeling in this case is an irrational guilt. It is the duty of the pastor when counseling such a person to assist him to overcome these irrational guilt feelings and teach him that animal emotions arise spontaneously in all humans. Much of the guilt that will be brought to the pastor will be irrational guilt.

2. *Rational guilt.* The second type of guilt is rational or moral guilt. Church catechisms maintain that this guilt may arise because of thoughts, words, deeds, or omissions. For a thought, word, deed, or omission to be "sinful," the catechism says it must be a serious matter which one knows is wrong and which one chooses to do deliberately.

Knowledge, freedom, and the seriousness of the thought, word, deed, or omission must be considered by the counselor. Before considering these, however, it is essential that the counselor seek to determine the certain conscience of the client regarding any matter he might consider cause for moral guilt feelings. To illustrate, again: A very devout and conscientious Methodist comes to a Catholic for counseling. The Catholic believes the Roman Catholic Church is the true church; the Methodist believes the Methodist Church is the true church. From the Roman Catholic's point of view, the Methodist has a certain but erroneous conscience. It is imperative, however, from the Catholic's point of view for the Methodist to follow his erroneous conscience because it is a certain conscience. From the Catholic's point of view, the Methodist is being a good Catholic by remaining a Methodist because he is living up to his conscience and he will be judged on the basis of his certain conscience even if it appears erroneous to the Catholic.

As teacher and educator, the ordained minister or priest attempts to help individuals form *true* consciences. On the other hand, as counselor the pastor must respect the *certain* conscience of the client whether it is, from the counselor's point of view, true or erroneous.

Assisting a client to form a certain conscience where there may possibly be feelings of moral guilt and culpability is the first duty of the pastoral counselor. Next, the counselor should assist a client in overcoming some kinds of moral guilt feelings even in what may seem serious matters when there is lack of knowledge or lack of deliberateness.

Factors Affecting Culpability

1. *Ignorance.* Ignorance may lessen guilt. Many acts performed by the mentally retarded, the brain damaged, and the psychotic may be serious matters, but for these culpability is lessened or does not exist. A psychotic patient kills another patient in a mental institution; there may be no moral culpability because he is not rationally responsible.

2. *Fear.* Lack of freedom and deliberateness can also lessen responsibility and culpability. Fear, for example, can lessen freedom and, therefore, responsibility. A woman was at home alone one evening; her husband was out of town. Late in the night she heard someone at the door. She became frightened and grabbed her husband's gun. All was dark; when the person opened the door she shot him. Tragically, it was her husband who had returned from out of town earlier than was expected. Morally speaking, her fear obviated culpability even though it was a serious tragedy for her. There was both a lack of knowledge and deliberateness.

3. *Force.* Force is another condition which may lessen freedom and, therefore, culpability. A woman is sexually assaulted against her will. She tries to free herself but is physically forced into a sexual act. It can happen that in this case of rape she may feel some sexual pleasure during the act. She need not feel guilt for this animal pleasure nor any moral guilt since she was forced against her will in the first place.

4. *Emotions.* Emotions—or "passions," as they are called in theology—attending actions often lessen guilt. The counselor, again, should remind a client that emotions as such are animal and irrational, but when they are so intense as to preclude the freedom to choose responsibly, culpability is diminished. A man becomes very angry and in his rage strikes a fellow worker. It is possible that this antecedent emotion may lessen culpability.

5. *Habit.* Finally, habit plays an important part in considering culpability. A man who feels guilty because of his habit of swearing

and cursing can be assured by the counselor that his habit lessens culpability—and that it may take a long time to finally break the habit. It is particularly helpful to an individual who is trying to break the habit of masturbation to be assured by the counselor that habit ordinarily lessens culpability.

In any situation in which a person's freedom to responsibly choose his behavior is limited, his moral culpability is diminished accordingly.

Having assisted the client to overcome his irrational guilt feelings and having assisted the client to form a certain conscience concerning his culpability and moral guilt, he will then assist the client to alleviate moral guilt feelings by appropriate action such as advising him to go to Confession if he is a Catholic, or to find some other appropriate way to feel forgiven and to overcome his feelings of guilt.

Values

In addition to guilt, the pastoral counselor is concerned with the values of his clients—personal values, interpersonal values, social values, and above all moral and spiritual values.

Values are standards or criteria by which an individual lives and by which he evaluates and judges his behavior and his accomplishments and determines his reactions to them. Many of his values are socially and culturally determined. Others are morally and religiously determined. These latter values are of particular interest to the pastor as counselor.

Values are not objective in themselves although they may be based on objective truths. They are based upon subjective truth or truth as it is known by an individual. Preferences, needs, interests, desires, objects, and goals all play a part in determining an individual's value system.

As educator and teacher, the pastor assists a client in developing his unique value system and particularly, he assists him in determining his moral, religious, and spiritual values. Further, he assists him in defining objectives and goals based on his value system. In his role as counselor the pastor functions differently. He assists the client with problems which may cause anxiety because of his value system.

A child is brought up in a very strict puritanical home. He is taught that it is not only wrong to engage in sexual activities but also wrong to play cards, to dance, and to engage in otherwise normal social and recreational activities. The child accepts these moral standards of his parents—he makes them a part of his value system. But as he grows up, he finds he cannot live up to the impossible standards he has accepted for himself—he becomes anxious and upset. He comes to the pastor for counseling. The pastor not only helps the client to develop a realistic and reasonable moral value system but also helps him set realistic goals and objectives within the system.

As it will be shown, many problems of human development arise because of feelings of inadequacy because one is not able, as a human, to live up to a perfectionist and unrealistic moral and personal value system. It is often said that ministers' children, as a group, have more frequent problems in later life than other people. Some find that they cannot live up to the standards set for them, and they feel they are no good and worthless because they cannot. This causes faulty personality development. A personality character disturbance known as an "inadequate personality disorder" may develop.

The pastor must assist such individuals to develop a more adequate value system. This will be the foundation for the client's mental health.

2

THE COUNSELING PROCESS

Introduction

There are many excellent books on counseling. No attempt will be made here to give an in-depth treatment of counseling and the counseling process. Only certain basic concepts regarding counseling will be delineated for the pastor.

Many pastors are afraid that they cannot be effective counselors. This is not necessarily true. Any pastor who loves people and who can learn to be a good listener can become an effective counselor. The difficulty comes in being able to be quiet and listen actively to someone else. It is particularly difficult for many clergymen to be counselors because they are more used to talking and giving advice than to listening. It is difficult for anyone to listen actively because this means that one must be attentive to all that another says, rather than passively sitting while another talks.

Listening is essential to counseling. To be a good listener one must not only listen actively to what a person is saying verbally, but also listen to what he is "feeling" and to what he is expressing by nonverbal communications.

A young boy was brought to a pastor for counseling because he had been stealing. The parents were very upset since stealing violated, seriously, the family's moral system of values. The pastor listened to the boy talk about his stealing. The boy did not know why he did it since he didn't need to steal—his family provided him with all his needs and gave him an allowance to use as he saw fit. As he listened, the counselor not only heard the words the boy was saying but heard certain "feelings" and pain the boy was communicating. Every time he mentioned his father, the boy's eyes darted to the floor and he seemed sad. This "heard" feeling led the counselor to ask about the relationship of the boy with his father. It was not long until the counselor learned that the little boy was lonely and starved for affection from his father. Unfortunately, the only time the father paid any attention to the boy was when the boy was naughty. Stealing had become a way for this lonely little boy to get the attention of his father. "Hearing" the feelings of this boy helped the counselor to evaluate the problem and understand the boy.

Or again, a woman came to a counselor because she was having trouble with her husband. She began talking about the way she had had to suffer because of his attitudes toward her. She said: "I have tried to be a devoted Christian wife and homemaker. I rarely go anywhere. I stay at home and do everything I can think to please him. But when he comes home he is moody and grouchy. He doesn't seem to want to be with me or talk with me—he just sits at home and watches TV or reads his newspaper. He finds every excuse he can to get out of the house at night."

The counselor tended to feel pity for the woman. However, he refrained and waited to hear her further. "I came to you," she continued, "because I found out today that he is seeing another woman and I'm sure he is carrying on a disgusting sexual affair with her." As she said the words "I'm sure he is carrying on a disgusting sexual affair," the woman squirmed nervously in her chair, crossed her legs tightly, and leaned both elbows on her stomach. The counselor perceived this as body-language—a nonverbal form of communication. He considered two possibilities—either the woman was insecure because of the consequences of the possible affair her husband might be having with another woman or, more likely, it related to her feelings of sexual inhibition—as if sex to her was "disgusting" and unpleasant. Because of these thoughts, the counselor listened to her in a new way as he waited to find out what this body-language meant. It turned out—after the counselor had spent several sessions patiently listening and observing the behavior of the woman as she talked—

that she was frigid, had a dislike for all sexual relations, and considered sex disgusting. Under the guise of being very pious and religious, she was able to avoid sexual relations with her husband. She had refused him sexual satisfaction for at least a year. In her own words: "I always give up sex for Lent and I expect my husband to do so too—in fact, it has been over a year now since we have had sexual relations. I felt it would be a holy, pious, and virtuous thing for both of us to abstain."

If the counselor had listened only to what the woman said in the first interview, he might have been tempted to sympathize with her and reinforce her self-pity because of her husband's abuse and inattention to her. It was the nonverbal communication as she discussed sex that led him to suspect there was more to her story and a deeper problem than a simple problem of a husband who was no longer attracted to his wife.

A good counselor, then, listens to a client in many ways. He listens not only to what the client says, but also is attentive to what a client may be feeling and to what a client communicates through posturing.

Counseling is a process; it is not something static. There are certain necessary elements and stages in that process. These are (1) the initial interview; (2) the counseling relationship; and (3) the terminal phase.

The Initial Interview

This is a most important stage in counseling. During this stage the client decides if he wishes to continue with the counselor and the counselor decides if he wishes to counsel the client and to what degree, if he chooses to counsel, he is competent to handle the person and the person's problem.

1. *The client and the initial interview.* The first interview with the client is critical for him. He may have come to the counselor reluctantly, filled with anxiety and apprehension. The way he is re-

ceived and treated on this first visit may well determine if he continues in counseling or not. There are a number of seemingly simple things a counselor can do to create an atmosphere that may help the client on his first visit. In general they involve helping the client feel comfortable, relaxed, and safe with the counselor and feeling accepted as a person.

The client must feel comfortable and be able to relax. To make this possible, the counselor must have a comfortable place for counseling, with comfortable chairs and a pleasant decor. In order to relax the potential client, the counselor must make him feel that he is wanted and that the counselor welcomes the opportunity to share himself with the person. Too often it happens that a counselor has decided he will watch his favorite football game even when he is supposed to be on duty; the doorbell rings—a person needs counseling—and he goes to the door and greets the "intruder" in such a way that counseling is not only impossible but the problems of the potential client are aggravated by the rejection he has experienced at the hands of the one who should give him pastoral care.

The time and length of time for counseling does present special problems to busy pastors. If he is busy, legitimately, when a person comes to him, he can make it clear to the individual why he cannot accept the client at the moment but offer to give him another appointment at a later date.

One of the most important aspects of counseling involves the length of time for a counseling session. One of the ways a person shows respect for another human being is to respect his time. Time for counseling is no exception. At the outset the counselor should indicate exactly how much time he can give the client and how often he will be able to see the client. If he can give only fifteen minutes, he must make this clear to the client. However, once having committed himself for a specific length of time, he is obliged to give the time to the client, be it fifteen minutes or one hour. He should not interrupt the client's time to answer the telephone, the doorbell, etc. Only in this way does the counselor show respect for the client. On the other hand, he has a right to respect from the client for his time. The client must be taught that he shows respect by keeping his appointments and by arriving on time for them. The client should not be allowed any more time for a session than the time scheduled. He should respect the time of the counselor and not impose on it outside of the counseling time except for an emergency. The counselor can, without endangering the relationship, insist that both respect each other's time. To do so will, in most cases, improve the possibility of an effective client-counselor relationship. It will improve the possibility of a comfortable and relaxed atmosphere for the client and counselor.

The atmosphere for the client must not only be comfortable and relaxed but also it must be safe. Safe, in the sense that the client feels free to talk about anything he wishes without fear of censure, reproach, or embarrassment. It is not easy for a married man to discuss the affair he is having with an unmarried woman. Often he will find it difficult and painful to discuss this relationship and the guilt he feels about it. He does not want to be censured or reprimanded. He does not want someone to talk to who may not only reproach him but also may expose his situation. Instead, he needs to feel safe, in that he will be accepted and respected as a person in pain regardless of his conduct and behavior and that he can talk freely to the counselor about his problems and his pain, without any possibility of censure, exposure, or being overheard by others outside the counseling room.

It is the counselor's obligation to create an atmosphere in which a client may feel comfortable, relaxed, and safe; it is, equally, important that he makes the client feel that he is accepted and understood.

"Empathic understanding" is considered one of the most important elements in effective counseling. Empathic understanding means that the counselor not only is able to infer accurately a client's feelings, attitudes, or beliefs, but also that he is able to convey in some way to the client that he is aware and understands. It means that he understands what the client is saying or feeling and is able to make it known to the client that he does understand. In those instances where he does not yet understand what the client is saying, he must let the client know that he is trying to understand.

A young woman comes to the pastor; she describes how she has drifted from one job to another—she drinks too much—she lives alone—she has no close friends—she doesn't go to Mass any more—she has not lived up to her family or her own expectations—she feels very guilty about her conduct and attitude toward life in general.

The pastor hears her words and also perceives a lonely and unhappy woman in pain because she feels isolated, unwanted, and inadequate. He may show empathic understanding of the woman by the simple statement, "It must be very painful for you at this moment; it must hurt a lot." He does not have to comment on what she says directly; he hears the pain and lets her know he understands what she is really feeling and really trying to say.

Empathic understanding implies that the counselor knows what a client is experiencing and feeling but that he need not feel the same way himself. To restate, the pastor does not need to experience the same feelings that the client experiences; he does need to convey to the client that he understands how the client feels and what he or she is experiencing.

Since each pastor has a unique personality, he will counsel in a unique way. In common to all counseling, however, to be successful as a counselor he must learn to listen, he must be able to create a comfortable, relaxing, and safe atmosphere for a client, and he must be able to empathically understand the client.

2. *The counselor and the initial interview.* The first session is a very important one for the counselor as well as for the client. The counselor must decide two things during the session or soon thereafter. He must decide if he is competent to handle the person and the problem of the person personally, in consultation with other professionals, or not at all. If he decides he has at least some competency, he must decide if he is willing and wants to serve as counselor to the person.

It is essential that the counselor determine as soon as possible his competency to counsel an individual who comes to him. One of the main purposes of this book is to assist the counselor in determining his degree of competency in specific cases. He must decide when he is competent to handle a person and his problem without assistance; when he is competent to handle the person and the problem in cooperation with or as a consultant to another professional such as a clinician, and, when he is not competent to handle either the person or the problem and must refer the client to another professional.

A man comes to the pastor because he feels guilty because he was legitimately away from home when his house burned down and his wife was killed; the pastor alone may be competent to assist the man to overcome his irrational guilt feelings. On the other hand, a woman comes to the pastor because she feels guilty because she is frigid and does not satisfy her husband's sexual needs; the pastor may help the woman to handle her guilt or he may jointly counsel or serve as a consultant to a clinician to whom he may refer her for treatment for the frigidity. Yet another man may come to the pastor and claim that he is God and has been sent to save the world; the pastor needs to recognize psychosis which he is not competent to handle and be prepared to refer and follow up the referral.

After the counselor has listened carefully to what a potential client says to him and observes the client's behavior, he must decide if he thinks that what is being said or is being presented as a problem only symptomizes a deeper problem. In many cases this is true. As it will be seen, for example, many neurotic reactions are caused by and are indicative of deeper personality developmental problems. The pastor is not expected to diagnose or treat abnormal and deep-seated problems of humans. He should not try to play psychologist or psychotherapist; it is not his profession. He needs, however, in a general way to recognize mental illness and the potential existence of abnormal problems in those who come to him, for many mentally ill or disturbed individuals come to the pastor before going to any other professional. The general rule of thumb is if a client is in any way behaving (which includes the things he is telling the pastor) outside or beyond the limits of what the pastor has come to experience as normal, he should consider referral. For example, a client complains that people are looking up his nose and seeing everything that is going on in his brain. He is anxious because of his lack of privacy. This is clearly outside the limits of pastors' competence. A man tells the pastor when he looks at attractive women, they explode and burn up. He feels guilty for destroying women in this way. This too will be outside the limits of most pastors' competence.

A man comes to the pastor because he feels not only guilty for neglecting his son but also because he feels he cannot be an effective and adequate father to the boy. The pastor may help the man overcome his irrational or rational guilt feelings for neglecting the boy; in all probability, he cannot help him overcome his feelings of ineffectiveness and inadequacy, which may be due to a deeper underlying personality pattern disturbance. In all probability he will need to refer the man to a psychologist or psychiatrist. He and the clinician may work together to help the man and treat his problems.

Ideally, the pastor will have available to him other professionals such as psychologists and psychiatrists with whom he can confer, consult, and often co-operate in the treatment of an individual. The pastor should get acquainted with all such professionals that are available. They cannot only assist him in dealing with clients but also help the pastor determine his degree of competency in the treatment process.

The initial interview is important to the counselor not only for determining the pastor's competency, but also for determining if the pastor is willing and wants to counsel the individual. It may be that he does not because of his own problems in relating with the individual, because the goals the client wishes to achieve are unworthy or distasteful to the counselor, or for many other reasons. He may wish to disqualify himself and send the client to other counselors. This is the proper thing to do in some cases.

Recently a man and woman came to a pastor for counseling because of serious marital problems. He interviewed each one separately. In the course of the conversation with the wife she said: "My husband is an airline pilot and is away from home a great deal of the time. I object to his being out of town and away so much. I insist that he get a different job and stay home. I want you [the counselor] to convince him that he must give up his present job and get one so that he can be at home every night." The man was then interviewed. At one point he said: "I am a pilot by profession and I don't intend to give it up. The trouble is, as I see it, I come home tired from a trip and I want to sit and relax but she won't let me. She wants to talk about the little trivial and unimportant things that go on in the house. She's gotten the children to be like her so that instead of leaving me alone when I get home, they are always pestering me for something. I figure my wife is at home, she should handle the children's problems. I wish you could make her understand so that I can have peace and quiet when I return from a trip."

It was clear to the counselor after the initial interview that he was dealing with two immature individuals who did not want counseling to improve the marital relationship and to determine goals, objectives, and values for themselves and the family, but rather wanted the counselor, by some miracle, to change the other party in the marriage. In this case, the counselor brought the two together and let them know that he could not help them and did not wish to take the case.

Sometimes a pastor should disqualify himself because of his personal likes and dislikes. For example, a few years back some pastors had a strong negative reaction to boys wearing long hair and beards. One should disqualify himself in instances such as this when preconceived prejudices threaten to thwart the counseling relationship.

The Counseling Relationship

If it is decided by the client and counselor after the initial interview to enter into a counseling relationship, a continued and sustained interpersonal relationship which is comfortable and relaxed for both the counselor and the client must be maintained. During this stage of the counseling process, goals and procedures must be set for the counseling relationship and techniques must be decided upon to use in the attempt to realize and achieve these goals.

1. *The interpersonal relationship.* A continued and sustained interpersonal relationship which is comfortable and relaxed is essential if the counseling is to be effective. It necessitates not only empathic understanding on the counselor's part but also a genuine respect by the client and by the counselor for each other and respect for the unique value system of each. It is impossible for anyone to be an effective counselor if he does not respect himself and his own value system; he cannot expect a client to respect him or his value system if he does not do so himself. Further, it is essential that the counselor respect the person and value system of the client and let him know that he has this respect. Again, it is not necessary for the value systems to agree. In many cases they will not agree. This is not important in counseling. It is important only that there is mutual respect for each other and each other's value system.

In addition to acceptance and respect, it is necessary for the interpersonal relationship to be honest. Great harm may be done by a counselor who is not honest with the client. Sometimes a counselor may be tempted to be dishonest with a client because he does not know an answer and is ashamed to admit his ignorance. This is totally unnecessary. A client will not lose respect or confidence in a counselor who admits he does not know everything.

It often happens that medical questions are asked of the counselor. A woman complains during the counseling session that she suffers severe headaches. She asks the counselor what causes them and what to do. The counselor is not a doctor; he should not try to answer the questions. He should honestly admit he doesn't know. Many times, to admit one does not know strengthens rather than weakens the interpersonal relationship between the client and counselor. Somehow it conveys to the client that the counselor knows his business and is competent as a counselor since he does not try to be some other professional.

In some fields of psychotherapy—notably psychoanalytical therapy—strong feelings shared by the client and the therapist are known as "transference" and "countertransference." This subject forms a large body of the psychoanalytical literature and forms a major focus of therapeutic activities. For the purpose of the pastor as counselor, however, he should accept the feelings in the counseling relationship as such and not feel it necessary to do something about them.

A client may express hostility or hate for the counselor at one time. At another time a client may claim to be in love with the counselor and may express desires for a more intimate interaction. It is very flattering to a counselor to have a handsome man or a beautiful woman declare that he or she is in love with him. The counselor should not be "seduced" or "compromised," that is, led beyond his usual way of behavior by expressions of desire and love.

2. *Goals and objectives.* Both the counselor and client have goals and objectives for the counseling relationship. In general, the goals of the pastoral counselor are to assist an individual to find more rewarding—more adaptive—ways to behave, think, and feel and to assist the client to overcome feelings of guilt and develop a realistic and appropriate moral, spiritual, and personal value system.

Specific goals for the counseling relationship must be determined also. Once these goals have been agreed upon, the counselor must decide if they are realistic and if they are worthy goals. If they are both, the counselor then selects the procedures and techniques to be used to achieve these goals. If he does not think the client's goals realistic, he assists the client in developing realistic ones; if he does not consider the goals worthy and he cannot change the client's mind about such goals, he may wish to disqualify himself as the individual's counselor, as mentioned earlier.

A man comes for counsel who has a very strict moral code but whose family are not living up to the dictates of this strict value system. He wants the pastor to counsel members of his family in such a way that they will see the necessity of obeying this code. The pastor feels this is an unworthy goal; the potential client will not change the goal he wishes to achieve; the counselor will not accept the goal and disqualifies himself.

Too many counselors and their clients set unrealistic goals which are too high or impossible to attain; others set goals which are too low and therefore do not meet the full potential of the relationship.

When some individuals cannot achieve unrealistically high goals, they feel inadequate and worthless. When others set unrealistically low goals, they become bored and unchallenged. A sister in a convent came to a pastoral counselor one day upset, discouraged, and depressed. She had determined that when she entered the convent she was going to become a saint by obeying perfectly all the rules and regulations of the house. Now, after a year, she was discouraged and disheartened because she had not been perfect. In her own words, "Why, I can't even keep the rule about meditation. We are supposed to meditate for thirty minutes at 4:30 A.M. in the chapel each morning. I try, but invariably instead of meditating I fall asleep."

Unrealistic goals such as those have caused discouragement and disillusionment to many sisters. In many cases it has made them feel inadequate and worthless. The counselor's task is to help the sister gain skills at setting realistic religious and moral goals. He does this by showing her how to develop realistic goals within the therapeutic process itself.

On the other hand, it is not uncommon that an individual sets a goal which is too low, even though it is a worthy goal. A young man with a brilliant mind was not encouraged to go to college and become a professional man as he would have liked to do. His father and mother had humble backgrounds; his father had worked in the same factory all his life. The family could see no use in the young man going to college; he could make good money working in the factory where his father worked. The young man was convinced by his parents that he should go to work and not to school. He did but he was not using his talents or abilities or functioning at his personal capacity. He became bored and felt useless. He turned to alcohol and drugs and to companions whose moral and spiritual values were lower than his. The pastoral counselor discovered he had a habit of looking to others for his goals and moral and spiritual values and taught him how to develop his own by doing this with him in the counseling process.

Helping the client find realistic goals and objectives, particularly in the areas of moral, spiritual, and personal values, is the unique task of the pastor. Assisting the client to find ways to achieve these goals is one specific goal of pastoral counseling and is pursued by the very activity of setting goals and achieving goals within the counseling process itself.

Counseling Techniques

Once the counselor-client therapeutic relationship has been established and the goals and objectives of the relationship have been agreed upon, the procedures and the counseling techniques to achieve these goals are chosen by the counselor. There are many counseling techniques. It would be out of place to spend a great deal of time in this book discussing and describing these techniques; there are many good books available which deal with this subject. In reality, it does not matter what technique a counselor uses, provided at the end of the counseling process the client's and counselor's goals have been achieved. A few of the major techniques or types of techniques will be briefly indicated. Psychoanalysis will not be considered, since it is primarily a technique for depth therapy and is not an appropriate technique for anyone without a medical degree.

In general, there are three types of counseling techniques—holistic techniques, which seek to treat the whole person rather than a specific problem; techniques which are concerned primarily with specific problems rather than the whole person; and techniques which seek through skill training to teach individuals to handle their own problems and be their own therapists.

1. *Holistic techniques.* There are many types of holistic counseling techniques. Four are of particular interest to the pastor. These are directive techniques; reality therapy and counseling techniques; Gestalt therapy and counseling techniques; and, client-centered, or nondirective, techniques.

a. Least useful of the four types of holistic techniques are directive ones. They have been popular in the past, especially with clergymen who did not wish to get personally involved with the client.

A man comes to the rectory or parsonage; he is having trouble with a neighbor over a question of who has the right to the fruit off an apple tree that is planted on his property but hangs over on the neighbor's property. Harsh words are exchanged and now they don't speak to each other. "What should I do?" he inquires of the pastor. The pastor, having consulted his moral books on justice and rights proceeds to tell the man what is right and wrong, what he must do, and precisely how to handle the guilt he feels for his behavior. Everything is done by the counselor; the so-called client simply listens. This is not a good technique for the pastor to use in counseling because the counselor assumes the role of an autocratic, authoritarian, infallible oracle. In reality, he ceases to be a counselor when he uses a directive technique and becomes instead an adviser or something other than a counselor.

b. Gestalt therapy and counseling techniques have become popular with many therapists in the past few years. There are many variations in Gestalt techniques. All, however, are based to some degree upon the philosophy that the whole is greater than its parts—the person is more than the sum of his individual parts. It maintains that as a person becomes whole and integrated, he becomes a healthier person and one better able to find adaptive ways to handle his life's problems.

A shy man is inhibited and afraid of the opposite sex. Possibly, through what is known as encounter group therapy, the man finds within himself sexual drives which need to be integrated into his personality. He is helped to find ways to express these sexual desires, to overcome his shyness and find someone with whom he can relate. Although this is an important holistic therapeutic technique, it is rarely used by the pastor in counseling. Ordinarily these techniques require considerable training and are more useful to psychotherapists rather than counselors.

c. One of the most commonly used techniques for counseling is reality therapy and reality counseling. Essentially, it consists of a dialogue between a counselor and a client usually centering around the client's past life and experiences. Reality therapy is based upon the philosophy that if a person can face reality, he and the counselor can find solutions for his problems. In order to face reality, the client narrates his life experiences and the counselor seeks to interpret them or help the client understand them in terms of objective reality.

A person with an alcoholic problem comes to a counselor. The counselor says, "Tell me about yourself." The client says, "What do you want to know?" The counselor: "I want to know all about you. Why not start at the beginning—where you were born, what was your family like, how far did you go in school, etc." As the client tells his life story, the counselor listens for any feelings that might suggest the underlying source of the present problem. The client says he is angry with his father. The counselor and client explore the reason for his anger. The client says he has harbored resentment toward his father all his life because his father beat his mother many times. Every time the father beat the mother, the client went out and got drunk "at the father," who opposed drinking. Later in life he got drunk any time he felt resentment and hostility toward any one. The pastoral counselor does not feel competent to help the man overcome his addiction but he can assist the man to look at his alcoholic problem realistically and to find more adaptive ways of expressing his anger.

d. One of the most important techniques for counseling, especially pastoral counseling, is a technique initiated by Carl Rogers, a psychologist, called "client-centered," or "nondirective," counseling. Although its origins are not Christian theology and philosophy, its philosophy is consistent with Christian tenets. Philosophically, it maintains that man has innately, within himself, the ability to be mentally healthy. The counselor functions in a completely different way in client-centered counseling than he does in directive counseling. The counselor says little; he listens empathically. His role is to help the client clarify his thinking and feeling, usually by simply restating what the client seems to be telling him. He serves, as it were, as a mirror so that the client can see himself as he really is and can recognize his problems. With the assistance of the counselor, the client can reorganize his true thinking and feelings and find solutions to his problems.

A young woman came to a counselor because she felt unhappy and depressed. The young woman was living in a commune with two other women and three men, she told the counselor. She looked to see the counselor's reaction to this revelation. By a simple "Uh huh" he conveyed to her the feeling that he did understand and accepted the fact, but did not go beyond mere acceptance. For thirty minutes he said very little except to reflect back to her the concepts she was stating in such a way that the anxiety-producing implications were explored and seen by the client for the first time. This continued for several sessions. Slowly the young woman began to see her own problem. Although she pretended to herself and others that she approved and enjoyed the commune living, in reality she was violating her own moral principles by doing so and this was the cause of her depression. The counselor did not have to suggest a solution to her. She left the commune and in time overcame her feelings of unhappiness and depression.

Client-centered therapy is based on the Aristotelian philosophy which postulates and demands a profound respect for the dignity, value, and uniqueness of each person. A person can grow into his full potential only if he is allowed the freedom to become his unique self. The control task of the counselor is to provide that freedom. The client-centered counseling technique has much to commend itself to the pastoral counselor. For this reason, much that is contained in this book is consistent with client-centered philosophy and nondirective principles and techniques.

2. *Behavioral techniques.* There are certain therapy and coun-

seling techniques which are directed to specific problems. A large number of these are known as "behavioral techniques." Rarely are these techniques useful or appropriate for the pastor. Most behavioral techniques are based upon behavioristic philosophies which are monistic, deterministic, and materialistic philosophies which view man as an animal and nothing more. In the second place, they are not generally useful for pastoral counselors because they require special professional training.

In many cases it is not necessary for the behavioral therapist and the client to establish any type of interpersonal relationship. In fact, in many cases the therapist need not be known or be a part of the therapeutic treatment. These techniques, when used by skilled therapists, have been shown to be valuable in treating certain specific problems of individuals. The treatment of phobias, for example, has often been effective.

A woman is afraid of snakes. A Freudian psychoanalyst might conclude that this fear symbolized the woman's fear of the male penis. The behaviorist would not theorize or speculate. To him the snake is a stimulus which causes a response, namely, fear. Various behavioral techniques may be employed to extinguish the fear response. Or again, aversive therapy has been used in an attempt to treat various disorders such as alcoholism. A man is given an electrical shock every time he takes a drink. It is the behaviorist's hope that the man will associate the unpleasantness of the electrical shock with alcohol, so that aversion to the electric shock will be generalized to aversion for alcohol as well. The success of such techniques for alcoholism is still in doubt and questionable. In other areas behavioral techniques have met with marked success, as in eliminating bed-wetting in children.

3. *Skill techniques.* There are those therapies and counseling techniques which seek to train an individual to be his own therapist and solve his own problems when they arise. The two most popular forms of these techniques are called "transactional analysis" and "rational emotive," or "rational behavior," therapy.

Eric Berne, M.D., a San Francisco psychoanalyst, popularized transactional analysis in his 1964 book *Games People Play*. There are many others who have adopted this technique. Essentially, transactional analysis seeks to teach an individual a skill. The skill involves learning to analyze one's behavior and the behavior of others in terms of behavior as an adult, a parent, or a child. Conflicts arise between individuals when the relationship as adult, parent or child is incorrect between two people.

For example, a man and wife are fighting constantly. She goes to a transactional analysis therapist. She learns the skill of distinguishing behavior and attitudes typical of the adult, the parent, and the child. She analyzes her problem and behavior with her husband and comes to the conclusion that she has created the problem herself. Most of the time she has assumed the role of a mother—a parent —toward him and treated him as a child, which he is not and dislikes. She now seeks to solve her problem and his by working to relate to him as an adult to an adult. Again, this technique will have little value for the pastoral counselor unless he receives professional training in its use.

A most promising type of "skill" therapy was called by its originator, Albert Ellis, Ph.D., New York psychologist, "rational emotive therapy"; it is called today by Maxie C. Maultsby, M.D., "rational behavior therapy" (RBT). Like transactional analysis, it will have little value for the pastoral counselor unless he has professional training in its use. It has been found, however, relatively easy to learn. It might be well for a pastor to look into the possibility of learning and using this skill.

Philosophically, it is based on the premise that thinking precedes feeling and that the antecedent thinking of a person determines what he will feel. Emotions are irrational in themselves. It is not inconsistent or incompatible with Christian philosophy to maintain that what one thinks determines qualitatively the consequent emotion. Skill training in RBT considers four main facts: (a) an unpleasant emotion exists; (b) the individual alone or with the aid of his therapist must work back to the event which initiated the emotional reaction; (c) to experience a negative or unwanted feeling, wrong or irrational thinking concerning the event had to precede the feeling, so the individual and therapist seek to determine what was this thinking; and (d) the individual must decide what rational and proper thinking regarding the event should exist; the rational will be felt subsequently.

A woman walked into the therapy room in a women's alcoholic treatment center just as another woman in the group said, "She is a rotten person." The woman went to another room and cried. She continued in this distressed mood until she went to an RBT counselor. He helped her look at the negative thoughts and irrational thinking that led after the event to her unhappy emotional reaction. Two of these thoughts were: "That woman shouldn't talk that way; she has no right to do so," and, "I think it is terrible for her to have such evil thoughts," etc. The counselor helped the woman substitute rational thinking in place of this irrational thinking: "I wish the woman wouldn't talk that way but she has a right to choose what she says." Further, "I got upset because I concluded that she has evil thoughts about me. But how do I know what she thinks? I cannot know what another person thinks. I shouldn't even try to figure out what she is thinking." Eventually, the woman replaced her irrational feelings, because of irrational thinking, with rational thinking. She felt disappointed that the other woman didn't like her. She concluded: "I'm not going to let it get me down." In this case, it turned out that the other woman wasn't talking about her at all but was referring to someone else when she entered the room.

4. *The pastor and counseling techniques*. The technique used by a pastor for counseling is not important, provided he achieves the goals and objectives desired by the client and the counselor. Ordinarily, the pastor will not use behavioral techniques that are directed toward specific problems in an individual. Ordinarily, he will not use the skill techniques unless he is specially trained. Usually, he will use one of the holistic techniques in counseling. However, directive techniques should be avoided whenever possible and Gestalt techniques cannot be used without special training. Reality therapy will be the easiest for the pastoral counselor to use. However, it would be well for him to study client-centered techniques and, if possible, obtain training in them. They can be most useful. They are philosophically sound from the Christian and other religious points of view. The emphasis on the uniqueness of the individual and the respect due each individual is noteworthy. The healthy concept that man has within him the potential for being happy and healthy is a spiritual value that ought to be incorporated in the value system of any pastor.

Termination of the Counseling Process

One of the most important stages in counseling is termination of the counseling process. It is the counselor's responsibility to recognize the time when the goals of counseling have either been reached, have been found to be impossible, or must be modified. In cases of modification the counseling relationship may continue but for different reasons and with different objectives. In the other two cases the counselor should terminate counseling in the proper manner.

Certain therapists and counselors prolong therapy long after it should have been terminated—sometimes, unfortunately, for mercenary reasons or personal reasons such as self-gratification and personal satisfaction. A sincere pastor may unwittingly prolong counseling. This may happen because of the "dependency" that may have been generated in the client toward the counselor during the therapeutic relationship. It is common for the client to transfer his dependency and dependency needs to a counselor. In some cases it is temporarily desirable, but the counselor must remember that one of the ultimate goals of any and all counseling is to help an individual to "responsible independence." Clients do become dependent on a counselor. The counselor must set as one of his goals freeing the client of this dependency as soon and as rapidly as possible after their goals have been achieved. He fails if he does not assist the client to a responsible independence. The counselor is a success when he is no longer needed by the client.

Knowing when to terminate the counseling process is not always easy. In some respects a counseling relationship is like surgery; a doctor does not discharge a patient until he is recovered sufficiently. A doctor prepares a patient for discharge from a hospital; the counselor must prepare the client for severing their counseling relationship. Regularly, the counselor should evaluate the progress of the counseling process. When he feels the goals have been realized insofar as possible or when the goals are clearly unattainable, he should prepare the client for termination. Two cases will illustrate when to terminate and when not to terminate counseling.

A woman came to a pastor because she felt guilty about her feelings of animosity toward a neighbor. The pastor counseled her and showed her that her feelings should not cause guilt since they were irrational. In time she overcame these feelings. However, the pastor enjoyed her company and allowed her to continue to come long after the guilt had been alleviated. He did not do his duty as a counselor no matter how mutually pleasant the companionship was. In continuing the relationship, he took the chance of aggravating an unhealthy dependency in the woman and creating an impossible and dangerous emotional relationship for them to resolve.

On the other hand, it can be very harmful to a client to terminate the counseling process too soon. A boy, for example, came to a pastor for counseling because he was disturbed and felt guilty for his masturbatory desires and fantasies. The pastor tried in several sessions to help the boy overcome his guilt feeling but was unsuccessful in his effort. It happened that the pastor dismissed the boy with: "You needn't come back anymore. I've told you a dozen times that you have no reason to feel guilty, but you don't accept my word for it. I can't help you anymore." Such a dismissal not only left the boy disturbed but aggravated a deeper problem, for now he felt rejected by the pastor as well as by others. In this case the pastor should not have terminated the relationship. Instead, he should have suspected that there was a deeper problem which needed to be handled by a clinician. He should have referred the boy and continued to assist in his counseling if requested.

Successful termination of the counseling process does not mean necessarily that it is the final contact of the counselor and the client. A counselor should leave the door open to a client to return, for reinforcement or to discuss any other problems he may have.

Conclusion

No pastor should be afraid of engaging in pastoral counseling. Anyone who respects himself and others and who sincerely loves other people can learn to be a pastoral counselor. He is not expected to engage in psychotherapy or work in areas proper to clinicians, psychologists, psychiatrists, social workers, or other professionals. However,

he is the only one competent to counsel individuals in certain areas
of guilt and personal, moral, and spiritual values. He is uniquely
qualified to do counseling in these areas. He should accept this responsibility and try to learn to be as effective a counselor as possible.

II

Pastoral Counseling and
Human Maturation
and Development

3

THE CHILD

Introduction

In this and the next six chapters, problems of human maturation and development will be considered, to prepare the pastoral counselor to deal with problems arising at various ages and to define his role in helping solve them. Problems of maturation are the normal problems faced by human beings as a result of physiological growth processes from the time they are born until they die. They involve genetic inheritance, mentioned in Chapter 2, as opposed to (but interacting with) environmental influence—the developmental aspect. They are the growth problems of the child, the adolescent, the young adult, the middle aged, the elderly, and the dying.

If there is healthy growth, human life involves a constant and chronological progression from total dependency as a baby through the revolution of puberty and adolescence, when a person seeks an independent self-identity and sex identity, into adult maturity when one adjusts his independence to mutual interdependence with others. In middlescence a person tends to readjust his interdependencies as his children are no longer dependent on him and parents upon whom he had previously depended, now may become dependent on him.

In the geriatric years, ordinarily a person has no one dependent on him, and he often finds himself dependent upon those who depended on him in the earlier years. In addition, one or more of the partners in a marriage will die during this period, eliminating his last interdependence.

For the dying, in many cases, the pastoral counselor is the only person upon whom they can depend.

The pastoral counselor has an important and special role to play in the lives of human beings at all stages of maturation. Goals and values, particularly moral and spiritual ones, must be defined and be redefined by an individual as he grows older.

The pastoral counselor either directly or in co-operation with parents assists in solving problems arising out of the growth processes of children and in developing their value systems within the framework of family value systems. The pastor is valuable as a counselor to the adolescent as he seeks to find his own self-identity and develop his own value system.

The young adult must choose a profession or life's work; the pastoral counselor is needed to assist the young adult in determining realistic goals and ones that are consistent with his moral and spiritual value system. Most young adults get married; the pastoral counselor has a particular role to play in assisting young persons to determine not only their fitness for marriage but also the spiritual and moral values that are essential to successful married life. He has an equally important role for single men and women.

The pastoral counselor can be of great assistance to a middle-aged person who comes to realize that he cannot completely achieve all the goals he wishes, and, therefore, must adjust his goals within his value system to more realistic objectives for the remainder of his life.

The pastoral counselor has a special role in assisting elderly people to adjust to the conflicts that arise because of the disparity between their moral and spiritual value systems and the value systems of their children and grandchildren and others they love of a different generation. In addition, the counselor must help them adjust to a world that frequently no longer finds relevant the moral and spiritual value system that they hold dear.

The special role of the pastoral counselor in dealing with the dying is to help them avoid the despair they feel from looking backward at the life they are giving up and to look forward with them in very positive ways into the future they are entering.

The present chapter will consider the child and the normal problems that may arise during childhood maturation which can lead to more serious problems of personality development if not solved.

Often the pastor will be counseling the parents of children rather than the child, personally. However, it is essential that he understand children and their basic needs so that he can assist the child, assist the parents, or assist both parents and children.

Understanding the Child

Growth is a prime characteristic of childhood—growth from the helpless dependency as an infant toward personal independence. Growth. Physical, intellectual, and emotional growth. If growth does not progress normally in all three areas, problems will arise.

For example, the child of a migrant farm worker is forced to go to work in the field by a poor, hungry family; the child does not get to go to school. His intellectual growth is interfered with because of lack of schooling; his emotional development is not normal since he is too young to assume the adult role of assistant breadwinner for the family. As the years go by, he becomes increasingly bitter and resentful; he becomes hostile and aggressive toward others around him. Because nothing was done for him as a child to give him a chance to develop and grow normally, personality problems result; he may become antisocial or become a criminal.

Or again to illustrate, a mother pampers and babies her daughter. The child remains dependent on the mother. The situation is never remedied. When the girl is eighteen, her mother dies. The girl is totally unprepared to stand on her own two feet. She develops an anxiety neurosis, which must be treated by a clinician because of her immaturity, dependency, and failure to grow emotionally in a normal manner.

Imitation is a second characteristic of childhood. When a child is born, he is like a blank page. When he is young, he learns by imitation. He absorbs and imitates the attitudes, mannerisms, and reactions of his parents. It is said that 80 per cent of what a child will be is determined early in life from imitation of his parents. By the time he starts to school, many of his attitudes, prejudices, and emotional characteristics are already formed.

A Gentile father constantly makes fun of the Jewish merchant down the street. His young son learns by imitation to be prejudiced. Conversely, a black mother makes her daughter's friends welcome in their home regardless of race, color, or religion. The girl grows up without prejudice and accepts every individual as equal to any other individual whether he is black or white, Catholic or Protestant, Jew or Oriental.

During a child's first year of school, however, imitation of the teacher and her attitudes is more important than the parents in personality development. After the child is approximately eight years of age, his peers, not the parents or the teacher, plays the major role in determining his personality development through imitation.

Many parents come to a pastoral counselor confused and concerned because a nine-year-old child is behaving so differently from the way the parents have taught him to behave. For example, a child who has never heard a curse word in the home has begun to use obscenities. The pastoral counselor must know that the major impact on the child's behavior after the age of seven is his peers and the influence of the family and its value system play a decreasingly important role in the behavioral development of the child.

Often a pastoral counselor must remind parents that a child's personality is determined more by how parents in fact behave than by their formal lectures on how to behave. To re-emphasize this point, the example of parents is critically important in determining the personality and growth of a child.

Fantasy is characteristic of a child's outlook upon the world in contrast to the more realistic outlook that must obtain for the adult. It is normal and good in a child.

A child draws a giraffe with three heads and colors each head with a different crayon. It sometimes happens that an adult who does not understand the child's world will tell him his drawing is ridiculous. Such an attitude may interfere with the normal growth of the child since the child may interpret this as punishing derision. Properly understood and accepted, the child should be encouraged by the adult, who recognizes that the child is using his imagination. Such divergent thinking must be encouraged if a child is to grow into a creative adult—which has strong contemporary value. In addition, a child should be encouraged to explore the limits of his imaginative, sometimes Alice-in-Wonderland world. By being understood and by being allowed to explore his fantasy world, a child may find personal interests and desires which will help him to determine future goals, values, and even a vocation. These may help a child decide if he wants to become an artist, a musician, a fireman, a policeman, a minister, a priest, a sister. That is, he discovers his interests as he, imaginatively, plays these roles.

Finally, parents and counselors should remember not only that fantasy—divergent thinking—is a normal part of the child's behavior but also that a child looks at the world about him synthetically rather than analytically. That is, the child sees the world in terms of wholes and wholeness rather than in terms of separate entities and parts. The analytical adult may go into a forest, see the trees, and estimate how many board feet are there and how much the wood is worth and feel nothing. The child will go into the same forest, see it in its totality, imagine the mysterious and magical things that must exist in the forest, and experience the beauty of the forest and the fantasies the forest has produced. The counselor and parents should encourage this synthetic outlook of the child so that the beauty he experiences in nature, in music, in poetry, in his childlike faith in God will be retained as values when he becomes an adult. The truly mature adult may have to be analytical to feed himself, but he never has to lose the synthetic outlook of his childhood and the ability to experience beauty.

Needs of the Child

To understand children both parents and counselor must recognize certain basic needs of children. Minimally, there are three classes of basic needs, namely, the need for security, the need for authority and discipline, and the need for freedom.

1. *Security*. The need for security is a basic need of all children. It is the form of love that they understand. To feel secure a child needs (a) certitude of being wanted and loved, (b) certitude of ap-

propriate and consistent affection, (c) certitude that he is understood
not only as a child but also as a unique human being, and (d) to be
given opportunities to achieve within his or her own abilities, limitations, and personality structure.

a. To be wanted and loved. No need is more critical for a child's
growth and normal development than the certitude that he is loved
and wanted.

Some years ago a young man came to a pastoral counselor after
many years of confusion and unhappiness. He told the counselor
that when he was eight years old he was sitting in the living room of
his home with an uncle. The uncle became irritated by the presence
of the boy and shouted at him: "I don't know why your father and
mother ever took you out of the gutter; they should have left you
there." The boy in his imagination assumed that his uncle's statement meant he was an orphan who had been discarded in the gutter
because no one wanted him and that his parents were being dishonest in pretending to be his parents. The boy went to his room and
cried, feeling utterly alone and abandoned.

At his age he did not think of going and asking his mother and father if it was true that he was not their child. For the next ten years
he believed he was really an unwanted orphan and had been taken
in out of pity by his parents. Later the Army required him to write
his hometown for a birth certificate. To his surprise, he learned that
what he surmised from his uncle's comment was untrue and that he
was the legitimate son of his parents. However, it took many sessions
both with his pastoral counselor and with the clinician to whom he
was referred to help the young man overcome the damage to his personality development that his feelings of not being loved and wanted
had produced.

b. Affection. In addition, to feel secure a child needs affection.
This affection should be consistent, appropriate to his behavior, and
shown by both parents. It should be consistent in that it is given
whenever good is achieved or evil avoided; it should be appropriate
to the age, place, and time; and, although it may take different
forms, it must be shown by both parents.

Affection should be incorporated into the reward system of a family. It must be, however, appropriate or it may be nothing more than
sentimentalism and actually harm the child. A mother who kisses

her thirteen-year-old son and makes a fuss over him in front of her bridge group may be being sentimental and not showing real affection at all but embarrassing him in front of the group. On the other hand, a father who, inappropriately, shows affection to his daughter when she is having a temper tantrum is doing more harm than good to the child by rewarding negative behavior. In other words, it is when the child earns it, and not when the parents need it, that affection should be given.

c. Acceptance of individuality. If a child is to feel secure, it is important that he be accepted as an individual, unique and exceptional. To understand a particular child it is necessary for the parent to observe, patiently, the child's special behavior and to find ways to communicate with him within his own frame of reference.

Earlier it was indicated that a pastoral counselor must learn to listen to a client; it is just as essential for a counselor of children to listen to what they say and to observe their behavior. For example, a counselor observes a girl talking to her baby doll as she plays house. He notes, however, that the child shows aggression toward a father doll by refusing to involve it in the play. Such behavior may suggest to the counselor that something is wrong in the relationship of the child and her father. Later, he observes the behavior of the girl's siblings under the same conditions and does not find the same rejection of the father. He can infer a special communication problem between the first child and her father, who is capable, apparently, of loving his children. All the children have the same father but because each child is different, the manner of communicating with each child must be appropriate to that child.

The pastoral counselor must be aware that very often the child and later the adult's attitude toward God is profoundly influenced by the learned response to the father. It should come as no surprise to the pastoral counselor that the adolescent who rejects God is the child who earlier felt rejected by his father.

d. Achievement. Finally, for a child to feel secure, he must be shown realistic ways to achieve according to his own personality and within the limits of his talents and abilities.

A man wants his son to be interested in basketball and become a star but the boy is not interested; he prefers to read poetry and study philosophy. Furthermore, because of his physical build, he would be

unlikely to become an expert at basketball in any case. The pastor
should encourage the parent to let the boy explore and follow his
own interests even if it means disappointment for the father that his
goals for the boy are different from the values and goals of his son.

Pushing children beyond their limitations was illustrated, tragically, in the 1930s. A radio quiz show demanded bright children.
Certain parents pushed their children and were pleased to have
them selected for the show. Unfortunately the show demanded an
incredible knowledge of a wide variety of subjects. The parents used
every spare moment to force more and more information into the
children. They succeeded in making their children into living ency-
clopedias. However, within fifteen years many had to be treated for
nervous conditions and mental illness. Even these exceptional children had their limits. When they were pushed beyond these limits
they became insecure. They became insecure, anxious, and neurotic
because they were not permitted to achieve, realistically, within their
own personality, abilities, and interests.

2. *Authority and discipline.* Not only do children need to feel
secure in order to develop mental and spiritual health, but they also
need authority and discipline.

Children need mature adults, particularly mature parents, to
whom they can look for authority. Since the child learns by imitation, it follows that authority and its mature exercise over a child
must be based on each parent's personal self-respect, respect for the
spouse, and respect for the child. The father who does not show respect for himself or the mother who does not show respect for her
husband cannot expect the child to respect parental authority. He
may fear the discipline used by such parents but he will never respect them as loving authority figures. It is loving authority he needs
to learn to imitate, since most likely, he will be a parent himself.

To illustrate, to the son of a policeman his father represented law
and order in his community. Personally, however, the policeman felt
very inadequate and worthless. Maladaptively, he released the tension and anxiety that this feeling of inadequacy produced by arguing
violently with his wife and beating his son without any reason except to express his authority over him. Unfortunately, the wife was
very immature, dependent, and lacking in self-knowledge and un-

derstanding. She cried a great deal and appealed to the son by asking him constantly: "You do love and respect me as your mother,
don't you?" In time, the boy lost respect not only for parental authority but also for all who represented authority, both civil and religious. He became antisocial and ended up in prison where he still
remains, a confirmed agnostic.

Discipline, then, like affection must be consonant with a child's
behavior. A child's need for authority requires that this authority be
exercised by appropriate discipline. Discipline must be exercised in
such a way that it assists the child to learn self-control, to control his
innate aggressive tendencies, and to eliminate behavior which might
disrupt the home or endanger his relationship with others and
society.

After many years of discussion with parents who have used authority wisely and exercised discipline effectively, four guidelines
seem to emerge as essential for success. These were: (a) rules must
be set up in a home after mutual discussion and agreement between
the two parents and the children when the children are old enough
to understand and discuss such rules; (b) after this agreement and
formulation of the household rules, the parents must be sure that everyone concerned understands the rules; (c) the rules must be
backed by both rewards and punishments agreed upon by the parents and children in advance; and, (d) critically important, discipline must be carried out by both parents according to the rules
agreed upon.

It has been found that families who follow these guidelines have
been successful in the use of authority and discipline. For example, a
doctor and his wife successfully raised seven children to maturity by
following these guidelines. Each week the doctor and wife spent at
least one hour with the children discussing and agreeing upon the
rules for the house and any modifications or changes that should be
made. In addition, in the kitchen of their home, there was a large
blackboard. Each week the chores of each child were written on the
board and anything else that might remind the children of the family's rules. The punishments agreed upon—such as not being allowed
to watch TV—were impressed upon the children. Equally important,
the rewards—such as going with the father to a football game—were

re-emphasized to the children. The children knew the rules and the rewards and punishments which backed up the rules.

The doctor and wife both admitted that the fourth guideline was the hardest to follow, namely, for both parents to consistently and mutually discipline. As the doctor said: "It is difficult to discipline a pretty little daughter who did not make her bed when she comes to you with big tears in her eyes. It took me a long time to learn that I would not be helping her if I did not discipline her and to learn that it was as much my responsibility to discipline her as it was her mother's." Similarly, the wife admitted she disliked to discipline the children and was tempted, often, to say: "Wait until your father comes home." She recognized that selfish and self-centered mothers often say this to children in their frustrated attempts to win favoritism from the children over the father and to avoid the stress involved in punishing a child.

When the pastor counsels parents regarding authority and discipline, he has a special opportunity to influence positively the moral, religious, and personal value system of a family. For example, he can counsel the family to make religion and religious activities a part of the reward system of the family. Too often, religion and contact with religious authority figures are used by parents as punishments rather than rewards. Too often one hears that a parent has told a child that if he or she is not good, the parent will take the child to the minister, to the priest, to the sister, to the policeman, to the school principal.

How different it was in a Catholic family which had lost its father. The mother would say to the five young children: "If you do your duty and fulfill your chores in our home, you will not only go with me to Mass on Sunday but I will let you go with me on Saturday as well." Two priests and a sister came from the family; the other children are happily married and devout members of the parishes in which they reside.

3. *Freedom.* From the moment of birth a child must begin his separation process, psychologically as well as physically, from the mother and father so that he can develop an adequate self-concept and personality structure to handle the stresses and strains he will encounter in life. One of the most difficult tasks of a pastor is to con-

vince a devoted and dedicated mother that she must free the child from dependence on her. If she does not, the child will remain dependent and immature.

To illustrate, a twenty-five-year-old woman came to a pastoral counselor because her marriage was in shambles. The pastor listened to her. The woman had been always, as she put it, "mother's little girl. I did not know how much I would miss her when Bob came along and took me away from her. I think I hate him. I want to go home." The woman developed psychosomatic disturbances, converting her psychological anxiety into physical illness. With the help of the oversympathetic, clinging mother, the woman divorced her husband and was welcomed back to the womb by the mother. However, it was not long until the pastor found it necessary to refer both the mother and the daughter to a clinician for treatment of their neuroses and the underlying problems of overprotection by the mother and the consequent dependency and inadequacy of the daughter.

To repeat, to counsel parents to free children from unhealthy dependence on them is one of the most difficult tasks of a pastor. And again, he must recognize that if parents do not free children from dependence, they cannot grow and develop self-concepts and personality structures that are necessary for normal, mature, healthy, and happy living.

The Child and Sex

The pastor is called upon often to teach and counsel parents regarding sex and sex education; many times he must educate a child himself and counsel the child regarding sexual matters. There are many facets of sex education of children. Two are particularly important to the pastor in counseling: (1) insistence upon respect for all aspects of sexuality, including the human body and its sexual parts, and (2) knowledge of when and how to educate a child in matters of sex.

No child is helped to achieve a mature sexuality as an adult by having the vagina and penis referred to as "ta ta" and "te te" throughout his childhood. In other words, proper names must be used. The pastoral counselor must be alert to any carry-over of the

Puritan or Jansensitic ethic—that consider sex and sex parts repulsive or the seed of all evil—in the attitude of the parents he is counseling. How much more important that the pastoral counselor screen his own attitudes in this area.

The rule of thumb must be that when sex parts are mentioned in the home, they be properly named. The same holds for other activities such as masturbation, intercourse, defecation, and urination.

An important task of the pastor is to counsel and instruct those who come to him that the human body is made by God and is therefore beautiful—including its sexual parts—and that sexual activities can be wholesome and healthy.

It is also important that the pastor know when and how to give sex education to children. If he does not give this instruction himself, he should teach parents how to do it. There is one simple rule which he and parents should follow, and a child will almost, without exception, lead parents and counselors in giving appropriate sex education if they follow this simple rule: Answer every question a child asks about sex when he asks it, answer the question honestly, but answer only what the child asks.

What can happen when this rule is not followed can be illustrated by two rather simple but amusing stories.

A little boy came rushing into his father's office and asked: "Where did I come from?" The father decided it was time for complete sex education of the child. He gave a long dissertation on sex, birth, intercourse, and everything else he knew about sex. The little boy looked perplexed and said, finally, "Gosh, that's something! The boy next door came from Ohio." The father didn't understand that the child wanted to know only where he came from geographically, not anatomically.

Another story illustrates the opposite extreme. A bright little boy was sitting with his grandmother and working at his desk as grandmother sat by the fireplace. After a time, the boy asked: "Grandmother, where did I come from?" Somewhat frightened by the question, she thought a moment, looked up at the chimney, and replied: "A stork dropped you down the chimney." The boy looked puzzled, stopped a moment, and then wrote something down. A few minutes later, he asked his grandmother: "Well, where did my parents come from?" Again she paused, looked at the chimney, and answered:

"Well, it took two storks to drop them down the chimney." The boy looked even more puzzled but wrote something down. Finally, after a long period of time, he asked her: "But, grandmother, where did you come from and my other grandparents?" She looked at the chimney. It might be a tight squeeze in the chimney but possible, and she said: "It took four storks to drop us down the chimney." The little boy looked even more puzzled. Again, he wrote something down. Finally, he went out to play. When he was gone, his grandmother rushed over to see what he had written on his pad. She was dumfounded and embarrassed to see that he had written: "I've learned a fantastic but disturbing thing today. There has not been a normal birth in our family for three generations." Clearly, the boy was ready for sex education but got instead fairy stories and lies.

To repeat, both counselors and parents have the obligation to answer the questions of children about sex. They must answer them completely. When they ask them, answer them honestly, but answer only what is asked.

Conclusion

Pastors and parents must know that childhood is characterized, primarily, as a time of physical, intellectual, and emotional growth. This growth depends on the adults around the child since he learns, initially and importantly, by imitation.

To assist a child in growing and developing a healthy personality and adequate self-concept, the counselor must empathically understand the synthetic and fantasy world of each child. He must observe and communicate with each child in his world and according to his unique personality.

The counselor must be sensitive to the needs of a child, particularly, to each child's need for security, authority and discipline, and freedom. He must understand that personality problems may result if these needs are not met.

The pastor must help the child to learn and appreciate the value system of his family and the moral, religious, and spiritual values of his church and society. This will help the child later in developing his own.

Experience has shown that many times the parents who bring a child to the pastor for counseling have the bigger problem. In such cases, the counselor should not attempt to deal with the problems of the child unless the parents are willing to be counseled also. If parents agree to such counseling, it is imperative that the pastor tell the child that the things the two of them talk about alone will not be told to the parents unless the child, himself, tells them. The pastor must inform the parents, also, about this arrangement.

If parents who bring a child with a problem agree to counseling for themselves as well as for the child, a time will be reached when the counselor may wish to suggest group or family counseling. If all agree—including the child—the counselor should not only assist the parents and the child with the problem presented but also should help them find and open new channels of communication. Lack of communication creates the most serious problems in human relations; most of the problems between parents and a child are basically problems of communication.

For the pastoral counselor, counseling parents and children together affords him an excellent opportunity to discuss moral and religious values and to assist the family in improving its whole value system and with implementing it in the home. A pastor, therefore, who not only assists a child and his or her parents to communicate more effectively but also helps the family define its moral and religious standards, goals, and values, will do much to assure healthy and wholesome growth and maturation for the child and, indeed, for the entire family.

her facial complexion or embarrassed by the obvious changes in her breasts.

Accompanying the adolescent's rapid physical growth is the development of the sex organs, sexual feelings, and very often exploratory sexual activity. At menarche, a girl's physical and emotional life undergoes a profound and lasting change. After his first nocturnal emission a boy may become not only aware of his sexual functioning but also realize that he is no longer a child and that he must in a short time assume the responsibilities and duties of an adult male.

Although the changes in the physical and emotional growth patterns of the adolescent are important to the adolescent, to the parents the accompanying changes in behavior are often even more confusing and disturbing.

A mother came tearfully to her pastor about her adolescent boy. She said to the counselor: "John used to be such a good boy, obedient and respectful to me and to his father. He enjoyed going to church with us and respected our moral values. Now, I don't know what has happened. He is only fourteen but he argues with his father and me, he questions what we say, and seems, at times, to be skeptical of what we tell him. Even worse, he tries to avoid going to church and openly stated the other day, 'I would rather go out riding with my friends than go to church.' He shocked me even more by stating: 'I'm not sure about all that religious stuff anyhow.'"

The mother began to cry. The first duty of the pastor was to assure her that there was nothing atypical about her boy and that his behavior was not unusual for an adolescent of fourteen.

The pastor explained to the woman: "Up to now, much of John's thinking and behaving was simple imitation of you and his father. Now he feels the need to throw off some of his dependency and think for himself. This applies to religion as well as other matters. I welcome an opportunity to counsel a teenager who says he has lost his religion but is willing to talk to me about it. In most cases, the adolescent has not lost his religion but is momentarily casting off the religion and values which he has learned as a child and which no longer work for him. He needs to replace his immature faith with a more mature and personal one."

The mother seemed consoled and helped. The counselor suggested that the mother let her son, John, know that he, the pas-

4

THE ADOLESCENT

Understanding the Adolescent

The time of childhood was characterized as a time of growth and dependency on parental figures, with the gradual emergence of an independent human personality. Adolescence begins with puberty and ordinarily lasts throughout the teenage years. It is the period in life when the normal child increases his efforts to be independent and to find his self-identity. Particularly important characteristics of adolescent maturation and development are growth, imitation, and curiosity.

Growth is as important a characteristic of adolescence as it was of the child. However, adolescent growth is characterized by critical changes in the physical, emotional, and intellectual growth patterns of an individual. Often these changes are confusing and disturbing to the adolescent. Often, also, they are shocking and disturbing to parents and to pastoral counselors who do not understand them.

Physical growth is phenomenal and rapid in the typical adolescent. The change in his physical growth pattern may cause the adolescent boy to be awkward and lose his co-ordination. Often it causes voracious appetites and creates a need for increased activity. A boy may be troubled by his loss of poise, the size of his feet, and the clumsiness of his whole body; a girl may be disturbed by changes in tor, would welcome talking to him anytime he might wish to do so. He cautioned her, however, not to insist that John come to see him for he probably would not consider doing so if he thought he was being pushed.

Perhaps the most disturbing aspect to the adolescent of the critical changes in his growth patterns is the new position in which he finds himself from time to time in regard to his dependence on his parents. He wants the freedom of independence, yet at certain times he wants the security of dependence. He is happy to be growing up, but he is frightened by this recurring wish to be free of his parents. One of the most difficult but most important skills for parents and counselor to learn in dealing with a teenager is assisting him to personal and responsible independence while still allowing him to lean and be dependent on adults without embarrassment or shame when he needs to.

A mother came to a pastor to learn if she had handled her teenage daughter correctly. The conversation between mother and daughter had gone as follows: "Helen, I've told you I do not want you to stay out so late every school night with the crowd of boys and girls you run with." "But mother," said Helen, "all the other girls in the neighborhood my age are staying out as late as I am; I want to stay out like they do. Why do I have to be different?"

The mother said to the counselor: "I saw that arguing with Helen would do no good, but when she ended by saying 'Why do I have to be different?' it gave me a chance to show her the consequences that could follow her staying out late each night. I showed her that it would not only hurt her grades in school, but also might undermine her health. I was pleased that she listened to my objections. Afterwards, we worked out a compromise. I told her she could go out on weekends provided she kept up her schoolwork and got the proper sleep during the week. She agreed. Now I want to know from you, did I do the right thing?" The pastor assured her that discussing problems with teenagers is the right thing to do even though the parent must be prepared to enter into a compromise.

Imitation was a significant characteristic of childhood; it is also a characteristic of adolescence but with one important difference. The child almost totally imitated the parents before he started to school. During the first year in school he began imitating his parents less and began imitating his teachers. The adolescent, in contrast, in his attempt to be personally independent of adults, ceases to imitate parents and teachers almost completely; instead, he now imitates his peers, which he began to do in preadolescence when his parents still had physical control over him. Now the parents have increasingly less physical control over his behavior. This is a major reason why peer relationships are so important in determining the adolescent's behavior and why it is important for the adolescent to have the proper peers with whom he can relate.

A boy would find it unthinkable to have short hair if all his peers in the high school had long hair; it would be out of the question for a girl to wear a dress to school if all her peers were wearing blue jeans. In a certain high school in an eastern city it was found that over 70 per cent of the teenagers smoke "pot." It would be difficult for parents and counselors alike to convince any boy or girl in the school not to smoke marijuana when the majority of his or her peers do so.

Popularity with peers and acceptance by the gang are also important to the teenager in that their reaction to him forms the basis for his newly emerging self-concept. Also, at least subconsciously, the adolescent realizes that they, too, are going through the same confusing changes and growth and are sensitive to the same things he or she is. Identifying with the gang, then, and empathetically sharing these traumas with peers can help alleviate the tension and uneasiness he or she feels.

The pastoral counselor must be prepared to tell the parents of teenagers that never again will they, the parents, serve as the major focus of imitation in the life of their son or daughter. Peers, henceforth, will be the models for all new behavior.

Curiosity is a third important characteristic of adolescence. Much of the fantasy and imaginative world of the child is set aside in adolescence for a more interactive exploration of the real world. This is particularly true as the adolescent becomes aware of his sexuality.

The desire of the adolescent to explore his own body and the bodies of others is even more common during this period than in earlier life. Commonly, adolescents masturbate and many practice mutual masturbation. The latter, usually involving members of their own sex, gives rise to the homosexual behavior common to this period of development. Much homosexual play during this time, then, arises simply from curiosity. It should not be equated in the parents' or counselor's mind with later exclusive homosexual behavior. Heterosexual exploratory activity is common also at this stage of development. While curiosity forms the basis of all sex play, the feedback obtained by the adolescent from the other person during sex play is all-important to his or her developing sexual identity.

Needs of the Adolescent

The needs of the adolescent are similar to the needs of the child. These are (1) acceptance and esteem, (2) authority and discipline, and (3) growing independence.

1. *Acceptance and esteem.* Acceptance and esteem from parents, counselors, other adults, and peers are essential to healthy and normal psychological growth of the adolescent. Acceptance is shown an adolescent by interest and respect for his or her uniqueness as a person. Esteem is shown by recognition of his positive achievements as the adolescent's new personality and behavior develop.

A recent movie told the story of an adolescent girl who committed suicide. She was the daughter of two performers in a traveling theatrical act. At no time did she have a life of her own or the respect of her parents as a person in her own right. Soon after she was born the mother carried her on stage and made her a part of the act. As she grew older she was made to dance and sing as a part of her parents' show. Never was she praised but, on the contrary, often criticized if her performance did not come up to the parents' expectations. Finally, in desperation, at fourteen she ran away with a man twenty years older than she was. He had no use for her as a person either—only as a sex object. When she became pregnant, he left her destitute and alone in a large city. She went to a bridge over a river nearby, jumped into the water, and drowned. Without personal acceptance and esteem, she had found it impossible to want to go on living.

To illustrate the other side of this point, a father had great hopes for his son. He wanted him to be a doctor or a lawyer. Instead, he

discovered his son was interested in cars and mechanics. The father
would have preferred to put away money for a college education for
his son. Instead, he bought the son an old jalopy which the boy
worked on constantly. The father showed esteem for his son by com-
plimenting his son on his developing mechanical skills. The boy
went on to become a fine mechanic and later a successful owner of a
new-car franchise. The acceptance and esteem shown by the father
to his son allowed the son to develop his personality according to his
own interests, resulting in a happy adult.

2. *Authority and discipline.* Authority for the adolescent must
be exercised with reason and intelligent understanding of the
changes, the confusions, and problems of adolescence.

The adolescent's world is like a football field, which should have
lots of room in it for him to move about in freedom but have side-
lines marked out clearly and a referee, the parent, to blow the
whistle.

Experience has shown that discussions between parents, counselors, and adolescents which include listening to and respecting the
ideas of the adolescent are the most effective ways to handle matters
of authority and discipline at this age, as they were earlier. When an
adolescent can talk freely with his parents about matters such as dat-
ing, nights out, allowances, cars, etc., the adolescent can, as a rule,
determine a goal system for himself and use self-discipline, which
eliminates much of the necessity for parental discipline.

In a midwestern town a few years ago, parents met with priests,
ministers, school teachers, and other counselors to discuss rules they
felt they should adopt because of growing problems with adolescent
discipline. Many of the teenagers were staying out all night; a large
number of girls were becoming pregnant; car accidents were frequent; and drinking among the adolescents was increasing. The parents met several times but could not decide on what they should
do. Finally, one very wise parent convinced the adult group that
they should meet with representative teenagers from various groups
and schools in town. A meeting was held and the adults listened to
their young sons and daughters. The adults asked them to suggest
rules to be adopted by all families. Surprisingly, the rules suggested
by the adolescents were much more severe than the parents would

have considered. All families agreed to adopt the rules. They became effective because the teenagers knew they had been consulted and respected as human beings in the formulation of the rules and agreed to abide by them because they had helped formulate them. Further, each tried to follow the rules in order to receive peer approval.

3. *Independence.* Independence is a third basic need of the adolescent. It has been said that adolescence is the bridge upon which the child walks from dependence to independence; at the end of the process, he must be a responsible, self-reliant adult who can make decisions on his own and who can make his way in the world while no longer dependent on the parent. He must now learn also the very complicated interpersonal roles required of adults in our society, including heterosexual roles, job-related roles, marriage and family roles, etc., if he or she is to achieve mature independence.

Earlier it was indicated that a child must begin to be freed from the parent from the moment of birth; it is essential that this process be completed during adolescence no matter how complicated and painful it may be for a parent or the child.

A mother and father talked their teenage son into seeing a pastoral counselor. This had been very difficult because of the son's intense need for independence from his parents and all other adults. There had been a complete lack of communication at home as a result of this need. For example, while the mother had come to the counselor to complain that the son was locking himself in his room every afternoon when he came home from school and masturbating excessively for hours, in fact her son had not been masturbating at all but had been smoking marijuana.

At the son's request, the first session with the counselor took place in the son's room in the basement of the home. The son stipulated that the parents must be completely out of the house during the session. To illustrate, again, his complete independence, the son broke off all conversation an hour later when he heard the parents' car arrive in the driveway. He refused to speak anymore.

In contrast to this independence, he was, on the other hand, totally dependent upon his parents for all of his food, his clean clothing, and even for awakening him in the morning so that he could meet the school bus.

The parents agreed with the counselor that they should not pry into areas that the son chose not to discuss with them. This was especially difficult for the overprotective mother. They should, however, maintain any family rules that had been agreed to earlier, while keeping open the possibility of renegotiating some of these later with the son as he felt the need.

How surprised the parents were a few days later when the son broke this independence impasse. He grabbed a butcher knife after dinner one evening and threatened to kill himself, while through his tears he screamed, "You don't love me. You haven't shown one bit of interest in me since that damn counselor was here!" This showed the normal vacillation of a teenager in terms of dependency-independency needs. By implication it also illustrates the very difficult problems and confusion this can cause parents. Needless to say, much work for the counselor lay ahead in this case.

The Adolescent and Sex

Had this book been written twenty years ago, it would have been a simple thing to tell the pastoral counselor and parents how to educate their adolescent sons and daughters in matters of sex. At that time, it was assumed that the teenager knew little about sex, about menstruation, spontaneous emissions, intercourse, pregnancy, and the like. The pastoral counselor would have instructed the parents to follow the rule: "Better to tell a child a year too soon than a day too late." In rare cases this procedure should be followed today for a naïve teenager; in most cases, however, it is outmoded and out of date; teenagers today are rarely naïve about sexual matters.

The adolescent gets most of his sex education from his peers. This is one of the reasons it is so important to educate the young child properly in sexual matters by answering his questions, answering them honestly, and answering them completely. By the time of puberty, his sex education by parents is, practically speaking, over. From puberty on—for good or for ill—he will accept sex education only from peers or from adults outside the home.

When an adolescent looks to the counselor for sexual advice and counsel, the counselor, in addition to following the rule given for children, should assist the adolescent to develop his or her own moral values regarding sex. Two things can be useful in developing these values: (1) helping the teenager have a healthy understanding and acceptance of the sex parts of the human body and of human sexuality, and (2) indicating to the teenager the consequences of sexual behavior.

A teenage girl came to a pastor because her mother sent her. "I can't see anything wrong with petting and necking, but my mother does and she sent me here to talk to you about it."

The counselor then discussed with her the potential dangers and consequences of petting and necking. He helped her understand that once a couple are stimulated and aroused sexually they are going to be frustrated if they only pet because of physiological drives to release this frustration by orgasm. It is not unusual at such times for the two to make a decision to have intercourse—a decision they would not have made had they not been stimulated so intensely by petting. In addition, many cases of so-called rape involve loss of control after stimulation by petting, when rape was not considered or intended originally.

The girl in question saw and understood the potential dangers and consequences of her petting and decided to avoid too much intimacy and stimulation, since sexual intercourse or mutual masturbation to orgasm would violate her moral code and value system.

Because the sexual learning of the adolescent is, for the most part accidental or haphazard learning from his peers; because in his sexual explorations he is confronted by a wide range of sexual behavior; and because the sexuality achieved by the end of his adolescence will, in almost every case, be his final sexual identity, human sexuality in adolescence is a very important subject. The next entire chapter will deal with the subject in greater detail.

Conclusion

Adolescence is one of the most bewildering and crucial periods in any person's life. It is a period which has a special challenge for the pastoral counselor.

The counselor must understand the critical changes that occur in the physical, mental, and emotional growth patterns which create a revolution in the thinking, feeling, and behavior of the adolescent. He must understand the importance of peer relations for the teenager and the influence his peers will have on his conduct and value system from adolescence on. He must accept, respect and understand the curiosity of the adolescent about the real world and about sexual matters in particular.

He must understand that adolescence is a time when a young man or woman begins to formulate his own moral, religious, and personal value system apart from the value system of his parents and other adults. The special role of the pastor is to assist the teenager to develop this value system.

Many teenagers feel excessive guilt during this period, particularly in sexual matters. The pastor must assist the adolescent to understand the different kinds of guilt and how to alleviate these guilt feelings.

To repeat, assisting the adolescent in achieving an appropriate independence, self-esteem, and self-confidence; assisting the adolescent in formulating his own moral and spiritual value system; and assisting him in alleviating both irrational and rational guilt are the special roles of the pastoral counselor when working with this age group.

5

HUMAN SEXUALITY

Introduction

It has been indicated that the pastoral counselor is concerned primarily about values and guilt. Since many of the guilt feelings of human beings result from sexual feelings and behavior, human sexuality and the guilt it causes warrant special treatment.

At the outset, it is important to remind the pastoral counselor of his special role. Further, certain basic principles of moral theology, which were outlined in the first chapter, should guide the pastoral counselor.

In his special role as pastoral counselor, the counselor is not concerned about morality as such; he is concerned about people with problems because of sexual feelings, thoughts, omissions, or behavior. For example, a farm boy comes to him who is performing sexual acts with a cow; the counselor is not concerned as pastor about bestiality and its morality; he is concerned about the boy for whom this presents a problem of guilt.

Four basic principles of moral theology must guide the pastor as a counselor in sexual matters. They have been considered earlier; they will be delineated again here for emphasis because of their relevance in matters of human sexuality.

1. Human emotions are animal and irrational; they involve no morality. One man is attracted to brunette girls; another man is at-

tracted to hairy males; a woman is repelled by dirty teeth; a man is repelled by women with mustaches. All of these repulsions and attractions are emotional—animal and irrational. In themselves, people's emotional reactions are morally neutral. As indicated several times, the counselor must assist the client to overcome the irrational guilt that emotions and feelings engender.

2. Not only are emotional reactions and responses morally neutral but so are all acts performed by humans—such as breathing—which are not considered, technically, "human acts." Human acts are those acts which proceed from knowledge and free will. Only acts which are performed with free will and knowledge have any moral content or should rationally be causes for feelings of culpability and moral guilt.

A man accidentally ran over and killed another man whose motorcycle went out of control in front of him; another man was taught that it was his duty to destroy men of a neighboring nation—he killed many of them. Both men have killed but neither of them are culpable. One did not commit the act freely; the other lacked knowledge that killing any human might be wrong.

3. There are two kinds of truth, namely, objective truth—that is, what a thing really is—and subjective truth—what one thinks a thing is. An orphan, for example, thinks he is the legitimate child of his foster parents; objectively he is not their child; subjectively he believes he is and this is his truth.

The standard for objective truth is God's Eternal Law and God's Divine Plan by which all created things are directed from all eternity to one supreme end, namely, to give glory to God.

The standard for subjective truth is an individual's conscience which determines what he believes is right or wrong.

A boy is taught that it is wrong to go to the movies on Sunday night instead of going to church. He decides it is not wrong to go. He acts accordingly. Whether he is objectively correct or not is not the question; he is not morally culpable because he is living up to his subjective truth.

4. Conscience—that by which man is judged by God—is consid-

ered, in technical terms, as (a) true or erroneous, and (b) certain or doubtful.

a. Conscience is said to be true, or correct, when a person appraised the morality of an act correctly in terms of objective reality, including God's Divine Plan and Eternal Law. It is erroneous when a person judges the act to be the exact opposite of what it really and objectively is.

b. With a certain conscience a person will know no rational reason to make him suspect that his judgment may be incorrect; with a doubtful conscience he has good reason to suspect that his judgment may be incorrect.

For example, a client's elderly mother was in pain and slowly dying of cancer in a home for the aged. He loved his mother. He decided to end the pain for her. He put an overdose of medicine in her drinking water when he visited her. She died that night. Most pastoral counselors would agree that the man was objectively wrong and had an erroneous conscience, but all must accept the fact that he may have acted in a certain conscience and that he had done what he thought was the best thing for his mother. If he acted in a certain but erroneous conscience, he would not, then, be morally culpable.

All humans, then, are bound to seek and form a true conscience in so far as it is possible. However, and this is the most important principle for a pastoral counselor, *every individual is bound to follow a certain conscience even if it is erroneous.* The counselor must accept the principle that every human is judged by God, not by His objective truth but by the subjective truth of a person based upon the formation of a certain conscience even when it is erroneous.

A young couple has decided on an abortion. They have sought, sincerely, to form a true and certain conscience about the matter. They have concluded that abortion is not wrong. No matter what a pastoral counselor thinks, he must respect the certain conscience of the couple and understand that God will judge them according to their certain conscience whether it is erroneous or correct.

The above is possibly the greatest source of conflict within a pastoral counselor if he sincerely tries to divorce his own certain conscience from that of a client. This conflict is further aggravated by the fact that there are many levels of credibility accepted for declarations regarding faith and morals—that is, for matters that certain churches and theologians say must be believed as opposed to those that may possibly be true.

For example, in the Roman Catholic Church some postulates are declared *de fide*, that is, "of the faith." A Roman Catholic must accept such a teaching, if he wishes to remain a faithful Roman Catholic, as objectively and subjectively true no matter what he might otherwise think. This became very painful for some Roman Catholics, including bishops, when a few years ago the doctrine of the Assumption was declared *de fide*. Nonetheless, the faithful Roman Catholic accepted the Assumption as true regardless of his personal opinion.

Also important are many teachings of the Roman Catholic Church which are called *certum*—roughly translated as "certain." Declaration of a postulate as *certum* does not mean at all that the teaching is certain objectively. *Certum* means that it is held by most theologians. An official teacher of the Church, such as a priest, may not disagree publicly with such a teaching. However, anyone, including a priest, may subjectively disagree, particularly if it seems the dictum is at variance with what he believes is true otherwise, including what he understands to be scientific findings and truths. At one time, for example, most theologians interpreted certain biblical texts as proof that the world was flat; obviously the interpretation and the theologians were in error.

While the Roman Catholic Church has a well-defined system of theological and moral dicta, pastoral counselors of other religious groups also fall under heavy restraints—although these restraints are not as systematically codified—when confronting questions of morality, particularly sexual morality, with their clients.

Some theologians—Protestant, Jewish, and Roman Catholic—maintain that any sexual acts not designed to procreate or not held within the bonds of marriage are morally wrong and reprehensible. Therefore, many theologians consider that masturbation is morally wrong and homosexual acts unnatural since neither lead to procreation or are not within the bonds of marriage. None of these postulates, however, have been declared *de fide* by the Roman Catholic Church although they are considered *certum* by most theologians.

Since almost every matter regarding sexual behavior is considered at most *certum* by even the most conservative Roman Catholic theologians, it is imperative that a pastoral counselor assist a client in forming a certain conscience regarding his sexuality and not approach him as if he were working with *de fide* declarations. The Protestant counselor, although given certain restraints by his Church, typically feels more freedom in these areas; however, he, too, must assist a client to a certain conscience in these matters regardless of his own interpretation of truth and morals.

Masturbation

In the not too distant past it was commonly taught that dire physical and mental consequences as well as moral damnation would result from masturbation. It is not uncommon to find parents and some counselors even today espousing such nonsense. This is the more unfortunate, because it is rare today to find a teenager who does not masturbate—at least sometimes. Preachments of serious consequences, physical, mental and spiritual, because of masturbation very often cause needless anxiety in human beings and may even cause serious mental disturbances.

Scientific evidence and research do not show that masturbation—as such—negatively affects an individual either physically or mentally. Problems because of masturbation are caused for those who still believe that it can cause physical or mental harm or believe in serious moral consequences if they do not stop completely. In other words, any problems derived from masturbation in reality precede the act of masturbation. It is these that must be worked on.

The pastoral counselor has four major tasks to perform in dealing with an individual who is disturbed by his or her masturbatory practices: (1) to help the client overcome fears regarding physical and mental harm because of masturbation; (2) to help the client form a certain conscience regarding the morality of masturbation; (3) to help the client alleviate any moral guilt that may be felt because of masturbation; and (4) to seek as a pastor to understand and help, in so far as possible, with any deeper problem for which masturbation is a symptom.

To illustrate, a young adolescent boy came to a pastoral counselor.

He was disturbed because he masturbated daily even though he did not want to do so. He was unable to control this behavior. The pastor first assured the young man that his masturbation would not lead to any physical disability or mental disorder.

It took somewhat longer to determine and help the boy form a certain conscience about masturbation. The pastor suggested that the boy could be forgiven by God if he felt he was morally culpable, but if he was certain in his own conscience that it was not wrong, he need feel no moral guilt. Several counseling sessions later the boy confessed not only that he did not believe masturbation to be morally wrong but also that he would feel strange and abnormal if he didn't masturbate since all his friends did. The counselor, regardless of his own feelings in the matter, accepted the boy's conclusion and his sincerity.

The fourth point above—that is, that a counselor should seek to recognize and deal, in so far as he is competent, with the deeper problems underlying frequent masturbation—may be illustrated by the case of a boy named Charles.

Charles felt sexually inadequate because a number of boys constantly laughed at him when they undressed together in the gym and taunted him because of his small penis. By innuendo they implied that because of this he was not much of a man. For this reason, Charles masturbated frequently mistakenly thinking that this would increase the size of his penis. This was seen by the counselor as an attempt by Charles to overcome his feelings of sexual inadequacy.

Homosexuality

Few subjects render many counselors more nonobjective and anxious than the subject of homosexuality. It is essential, however, that a pastoral counselor accept and respect a person who wants to talk to him about his homosexual feelings or behavior. He will be helped in maintaining his objectivity and feelings of acceptance of the client if he keeps in mind the following concepts:

1. Biologically and psychologically, a human may be considered "pansexual," that is, that the human being is sexually stimulated by countless stimuli not only from humans of both sexes but also by

other animals and even inanimate objects. In addition, homosexual attractions and behavior are conditions that mankind shares in common with all other animals. Such attractions and expressions of homosexual interests in humans are considered often contrary to the "norm" or "average," but in no way can they be considered "unnatural." In fact, according to the Kinsey reports of the 1950s, homosexual attractions, expressions, and interests cannot even be considered contrary to the norm, or average, much less abnormal or unnatural. The assertion by some moral theologians that homosexual attractions and homosexual acts are contrary to nature is scientifically not true for humans or other animals, the question of procreation notwithstanding.

2. Emotionally, human beings are neither heterosexual or homosexual but in varying degrees bisexual. Voluminous scientific literature exists today which indicate this to be true. For example, in a woman's prison 80 per cent of the women who, before incarceration, had engaged exclusively in heterosexual relations were now involved in exclusively homosexual relations. Or again, a navy officer was disturbed that a large number of males who had contended they were not homosexual when they enlisted were enjoying homosexual relations on the ship.

In one all-male theological seminary, twelve students were examined by a psychologist and the seminary rector before admission. All agreed that they had no homosexual interests. Within two years, a subsequent study showed, eight of the twelve were involved in homosexual activities.

3. The overwhelming scientific evidence, then, indicates not only that homosexual attractions are not unnatural but also that all humans, under many circumstances, can enjoy physical, emotional, and sexual relations with members of either sex, although there may be constitutional or learned factors which increase the probability of a stronger attraction to one sex or the other. Moreover, all psychologists know some kinds of learning can turn off totally a given individual from any sexual interest in his own or the opposite sex or both. More often those aspects that he is turned off to—that is, not experiencing—creates a person's true sexual problems.

Pastoral Counseling and Homosexuality

There are at least four homosexuality-related types of problems that people bring to the pastoral counselor: (1) problems for those who feel they are homosexual and who are disturbed by these feelings even though they are not acting out these feelings; (2) problems for those who are behaving overtly homosexually and who are disturbed by their homosexual behavior and interests; (3) problems for those who believe in homosexual or heterosexual monogamy but who violate a relationship with homosexual activities outside of such a relationship; and (4) problems for those who overtly act out their homosexual interests but who are not disturbed by this behavior and come to the counselor for counseling regarding other problems.

1. A married woman in an influential position in the government came to the pastor about her guilt feelings; she found herself sexually attracted to the female dean of women at a school she visited frequently. The pastor helped her overcome her irrational guilt feelings for this normal human attraction to a person of her own sex by helping her to see that there was no morality involved in attraction as such. The woman went away satisfied.

2. A married man who was disturbed by the fact that he went to male baths and engaged in homosexual acts came to a counselor. It was clear to both that he was violating his conscience. Since the counselor was a Roman Catholic priest and the client a Roman Catholic who seemed truly contrite for violating his moral value system, confession became the means to alleviate the guilt that he felt.

3. An Irish woman and an English woman had lived together, they said, "as man and wife," for fifteen years. The two were convinced there was nothing wrong in living together and having sexual relations with each other. However, the woman who came for counseling was disturbed and felt guilty because she had engaged in sexual relations with a different woman the week before. To the best of his ability the counselor sought to know the certain conscience of the woman. He concluded that she felt guilty only when she was

untrue to the woman with whom she had been living. Subsequently, he helped the client find a way to alleviate the guilt she felt for being, from her point of view, untrue to the woman with whom she had lived for years.

4. A clergyman served as a counselor to another clergyman who admitted openly that he engaged in homosexual behavior regularly and frequently. These homosexual activities caused no problem for the client. He had come to the counselor because of another problem —the problem he was having with his parish council and the conflict of their respective value systems. The pastoral counselor accepted the clergyman as a client and worked with him solely on the client's communication problem with his parishioners.

As in other areas of sexual counseling, the pastor has certain obligations here: (1) he must assist an individual to overcome his irrational guilt about homosexual desires and attractions; (2) he must assist a person to form a certain conscience regarding homosexual involvement; and (3) he must assist the client to find ways to alleviate his feelings of guilt and culpability for homosexual acts, thoughts, or desires which he considers morally wrong.

And again, it is necessary for the counselor to maintain his objectivity and work on the problem presented and as experienced by the client and not the counselor.

As a final example, a prisoner came to the prison's chaplain on the day he was being released from prison. He was heartbroken because for five years he had noticed that everyone in his cell block seemed to have a homosexual partner but him. The day before he came to the counselor he had begged, tearfully, an older inmate to have sexual relations with him so that he would not have to go through life feeling abnormal and unwanted. In his attempt to have sex with the acquiescent older prisoner, the client could not maintain his erection. His last chance had been a total failure and it was grief from this failure, rather than homosexuality, that brought him to the counselor. Clearly, objectivity on the part of the prison chaplain was required.

Pastoral Counseling and Heterosexuality

Most problems brought to a pastor involve heterosexual interests and behavior. Because the pastor is, ordinarily, more comfortable with heterosexual problems, we are considering heterosexuality and the pastoral counselor after discussing the pastor's relation with those who masturbate or have problems because of homosexual interests and behavior. Also what has been said regarding counseling those who masturbate or about those who have homosexually related problems is applicable to those who have problems because of their heterosexual interests and behavior. Often he must go further into counseling regarding sexuality when problems of heterosexuality arise, for often they involve feasibility and desirability of marriage and the potential consequences heterosexual relations may involve in or outside of marriage.

For example, an adolescent couple feeling uneasy about their sexual relationship came to their pastor. It was a month before they were to graduate from high school. Although neither had a job yet, both were optimistic about getting them and were planning their marriage for the week after school was out. The counselor understood that their sexual involvement with each other was not this couple's primary problem and that other problems existed—financial, vocational, etc.—which needed the attention of the counselor.

Unlike counseling individuals who masturbate or commit homosexual acts, the counselor should consider with a client who is proposing or is engaged in heterosexual activities outside of marriage the potential consequences of such actions including the possibility of pregnancy of the woman involved. In many cases the pastor will, as a sex educator rather than as counselor, instruct individuals and couples in such matters. In many cases it will be his specific task to assist clients in defining moral and spiritual values regarding marriage and family life. In every case it will be his task to help a client find and develop values in regard to his or her sexuality.

6

THE YOUNG ADULT

Understanding the Young Adult

When the adolescent revolution for independence subsides and the young adult finds he cannot live totally independent of other human beings, the normally long period of adulthood begins. For the rest of his life an individual must adjust, and often readjust, his independence and the mutual interdependence that he will discover necessary and that must exist between him and other people. This can be a difficult learning experience for a new adult.

A young man living in New York wanted to write a musical comedy. He thought he could do it alone without any person's help. He tried many times without success. He found he could write the lyrics but not the music. Similarly, another young man was interested in producing a musical comedy, but he could write the music but not the lyrics. A mutual friend brought them together; they combined their talents and became famous on Broadway for their shows.

Another very common problem of interdependence is that encountered by the young adult when he discovers he must adjust his independence throughout his adult life to various bosses—parental surrogates.

Three chief adjustment or developmental problems of the young adult involve (1) occupational choices, (2) interpersonal relations, and (3) personal value systems.

1. *Vocation* is a chief concern of the young adult. He seeks to find satisfying vocational outlets consistent with his talents and interests. This is a real problem during the twentieth century because of the wide variety of interests that many young people have today and the numerous kinds of outlets for each of these interests.

Another problem derives from the late age at which contemporary young adults enter their final occupational fields because of the increasing number of years of education required of them. It was not surprising when a large state university recently found that 70 per cent of its graduating seniors had changed their major after their sophomore year. It should not be surprising when the pastoral counselor finds numbers of young people—even some with college degrees —coming to him with problems of occupational choice.

In other cases the pastoral counselor may be asked to assist an individual in evaluating his abilities and limitations so that he can readjust his occupational goals when necessary. This was true for a young professional football player. He had been in a car accident and was taken to the hospital where it was necessary to amputate his leg. He was not able to play football again. The nurse, serving as his counselor, not only assisted the young man to overcome his bitterness toward God and people but also to seek another vocation. With her encouragement, he went back to college. Later he became a successful teacher of physical education in a junior high school and thoroughly enjoyed his work.

2. *Interpersonal relations* are important to the young adult. One of the major interpersonal problems of the majority of young adults is determining whom they want to spend the rest of their lives with within marriage.

Peers do not cease to be important for the young adult and for his interpersonal relations. In fact, much of the joy and pleasure he derives out of life as an adult depends on whom he chooses to relate with and the nature of the relationship. Just as there is an ever-increasing number of occupations a young adult may pursue, there is a wide variety of interpersonal relationships possible in our current society. In occupational matters *today* it is no longer given that the son grows up to enter his father's occupation; neither will his interpersonal relationships today be confined to those who live on

ouragement by others is ordinarily essential if a human is to
s full potential and satisfy his basic needs for self-esteem
esteem of others. In general, the pastor can help a client
imself if he shows him sincere and honest respect as
No matter how poor a person may be or how he may have
fail in life, he will not lose his self-esteem if he is re-
d encouraged by people who are important to him.

ample, a minister had a rather poor family in his congre-
he man was uneducated and worked in a filling station
could find a job. His wife was a plain but pleasant woman.
l four children and she was pregnant again. The pastor
how the couple fed themselves and their children. More
, he wondered how they could remain as cheerful as they
h all the problems and difficulties they faced daily. Even
wondered how the father's need for self-esteem could possi-
et. The minister, therefore, asked the wife how the family
d their happiness. She told him: "It's because Ted and I
other and the children. We know that if we stick together,
e it. And, as far as I'm concerned, Ted is the greatest man
orld and I tell him so every day. Sure, we've had some
aks, but I know we'll make it yet—he's got good stuff in

his type of encouragement, it was understandable why Ted
e up and was able to maintain his self-esteem. Even though
ad seven jobs in four years, the wife still respected and
n him and let him know it.

feeling of loneliness is a feeling that many people dread.
y the pastor finds himself dealing with his client's feeling
ess. The pastor has a special responsibility to help with
blems since they may lead to despair, the loss of faith in
His Goodness—they may even lead to suicide.
ral, all pastoral counselors attempt to help lonely people
hey are wanted and loved by others and are loved and im-
the eyes of an understanding God. A pastoral counselor
aware, however, that these counsels may be insufficient to
he loneliness felt by the client. He must understand th
g of loneliness a client has does not come from being alo

his block or those on a church committee with him. For example, in
this day and age, a woman may find herself playing one set of interpersonal roles at the office, another one with her girl scout troop, still
another one in her church, and perhaps, quite a different one with
the neighbors she vacations with in the summertime. It is no longer
unusual for a young person to come to a pastoral counselor complaining that he no longer knows who he is. He seems to be floating
through life and feels he has not really found himself as a "real" or
"genuine" person. Such traumas are known, roughly, as "identity
crises," because an individual thinks he must choose only one "role"
as the real self.

The pastoral counselor should help a person recognize that every
interpersonal relationship is a facet of his real self. The problem is
not the roles but the lack of an underlying value system with sup-
porting goals which organize these roles into an integral personality
whole. Such goals and values are invariably lacking in those who
complain of identity crises. The counselor's specific task, then, is to
avoid being tricked into helping a client find a specific interpersonal
role or roles, but should attack the more generic problem and help
the client define his goals and value system. These must of necessity
reflect his moral and spiritual values. The pastoral counselor may discover, frequently, that these latter are the most generic problems of
all.

Another large category of problems of this age group derives from
habits which are often carried over from adolescence concerning
adaptive and creative use of free time. For example, the adolescent,
having an intense need for peer approval, frequently comes to feel
that any time spent alone signifies that he is unpopular and, by ex-
tension, unacceptable to his peers.

The young adult often finds that he has carried over this way of
thinking into his adult life and now finds he is filled with anxiety if
all of his free time is not spent relating with other people even in
shallow, unmeaningful ways. The pastoral counselor's major role
here is to teach creative use of free time in which the young adult
discovers and explores himself by interacting with objects—clay,
wood, paint—and by interacting with ideas—great novels, philosoph-
ical writings, or even theological and spiritual literature—in addition to people.

3. *The personal value system* and its development is a third basic interest of the young adult. As a child he began by accepting for himself what he thought was the value system of his parents; during adolescence he sought to emancipate himself from this system and, if all went well, began to form his own. The adult must, finally, grow into his own independent value system if he is to live as a mature and healthy individual. The pastor should be concerned with assisting him particularly to determine his own personal moral and religious values and goals.

A twenty-five-year-old woman came to a pastoral counselor upset and extremely anxious. All her life she had lived sequestered from the world in the home of her mother, who had been a widow for fifteen years at the time her daughter came for counseling. The woman had never developed her own system of values. As she said in one of the counseling sessions: "I've always done what Mommy [sic] said to do. I've never had to try to figure out what is right and wrong; Mommy has always told me." She paused and began to shake nervously: "Now everything is terrible and I'm scared. Mommy broke her hip and may not be able to walk again. As if that wasn't enough, the money has run out that Papa left for our support. Mommy can't work so I've got to get a job—and—I just don't know which way to turn. I've heard so many horrible things that sometimes happen to young girls out there and I don't think I could stand it if any of those things happened to me."

With the assistance of the pastor, the woman found a job in which she said she felt safe. However, she developed headaches every time she was asked to make some minor decision on her job. It was necessary to refer the woman to a psychologist for psychotherapy. However, the pastor continued counseling the woman in conjunction with her psychotherapist, not only to help her develop self-confidence and self-esteem but also to enable her to work out a value system of her own, including moral and spiritual values.

Many times value systems achieved by an adult must be redefined and altered one or more times. For example, a man whose wife died had always wanted to be a Roman Catholic priest. With the help of counseling, he decided to sell his home and enter a seminary. Ultimately, he was ordained. His basic moral and spiritual values had not changed but his entire value system with its new goals and ob-

jectives had to be altered now that h

Another and perhaps more typica
Barbara, who came to her pastor fe
underlying feeling of guilt. She tol
ways wanted to help the unfortuna
deprived of the things she felt every
get better medical care for the India
children in Appalachia, cleaner ai
Harlem, etc. In short, her youthful
allow no one to suffer.

She went on to explain how she
various activities on various fund-ra
problems still remained in America.
she came to the realization that her
ing every evening and all day Satu
plaining of boredom when she turne
own family were not living a creativ
conflict for her. How could she dr
Appalachia, and yet how could she
own children things more important
live happy lives? She could see no
this impossible choice confronted h
stopped her activities outside the
The counselor's task was to help he
earlier goals in view of the later on
taught her that her goals and values
ing experience.

Needs of th

Earlier it was pointed out that t
human beings. Among these are ph
ity are personal and interpersonal n
be called upon to counsel young a
met, especially the needs for love, s
In practice, these are often express
agement and the painful need to avo

1. *En*
realize
and the
esteem
a person
seemed
spected
For e
gation.
when h
They h
wondere
than tha
were, w
more, he
bly be r
maintain
love eac
we'll ma
in the
tough b
him."
With
never ga
he had
believed

2. *Th*
Frequen
of loneli
these pr
God and
In ge
feel that
portant
must be
assuage
the feeli

—in fact, some people feel their loneliness most keenly when in a crowd. Instead, he must understand that loneliness derives directly from the absence of shared interpersonal love. Without shared interpersonal love, the feeling of loneliness is hard, if not impossible to dissipate in clients, even though they feel confident that God loves them.

Individuals with problems of loneliness come from all walks of life. The loneliness felt by many housewives who must stay home all day while their husbands are at work and their children at school is so frequently brought to the pastor that it warrants special attention. One counselor in such a case called in the husband and suggested that much of his wife's loneliness could be eliminated if the man followed the rule of the "three A's": show her appreciation, give her attention, and consistently and constantly share affection with her.

This worked for her, as well as for a woman, named Hattie, and her family who lived across the street from the rectory. Although she was at home a great deal of the time alone, she never appeared lonely. The reason was that her husband, Joe, never let her feel so. He worked hard as a welder in a factory in a city sixty-five miles away and commuted by train each day to his job. When he went to work and she had gotten the children off to school, Hattie spent her day baking, sewing for her family, and keeping the family's modest home clean.

Except to go to church on Sunday, Hattie stayed home. She had no money for a car and no interest in social activities such as bridge or bingo. Rarely did she get a new dress, but she kept the one or two she had made herself spotlessly clean even though she had to wash them by hand. Hattie looked forward to the evening. Every night when Joe came home she would be standing in the doorway waiting for him. Although he might be greasy and dirty, he always gave her a hug and a big kiss before he and Hattie went into the house. Never in the ten years the counselor observed them did Joe fail to give this attention and affection to Hattie. This was his way of sharing love with Hattie, which kept her from feeling loneliness during all the days she spent alone throughout the years.

Counseling the Adult Before Marriage

Giving premarital instructions regarding marriage, its obligations, and its privileges is the special field of the marriage counselor as apart from pastoral counseling as such. However, the pastor as counselor may be helpful to a couple in deciding (1) if they are mature enough to marry, (2) if they are willing to accept the limitations of the roles of husband and wife and, possibly, the roles of parents, and (3) if they are capable of sharing mutual love.

For many people the serious consideration of marriage brings unresolved fears to the surface, as the following illustrations will demonstrate.

A young woman came to the pastor in some distress because she and her boy friend had been considering marriage. She had a secret dread of marriage because, as she said: "I heard mother screaming in the bedroom when she gave birth to my little sister and I am terrified of getting married to Fred and the pregnancy it will invariably entail, as much as I love him otherwise." Clearly her attitudes toward pregnancy and having children was of great concern to her. The counselor might well find himself acting as a teacher if only to refer this case to some other professional.

An illustration of immaturity that would likely prevent a successful marriage came to the attention of a pastoral counselor one day when a young man complained that his girl friend had impossibly prudish ideas about sex. His own certain conscience appeared to be that once a couple was married, there should be absolutely no restraints on sexual activities. Specifically, he had made elaborate notes on various sexual activities that he had found described on restroom walls. He informed his girl friend that it was his intention that they engage in every one of them after they were married. She found it impossible to agree. He had come to the pastoral counselor demanding that the pastor talk her into it. Clearly, the man was, psychosexually, not mature enough to enter into a mature marital relationship.

Understanding "roles" in life and the limitations they place on individual freedom is necessary for all mature human beings, especially those contemplating marriage. It is important, therefore, that a counselor emphasize the limitations that the role of husband or wife will place upon a man or woman if they marry. To illustrate, if a young man wishes to accept the role of husband to a particular young woman, he must also accept the accompanying fact of monogamy. For another example, a woman may wish to marry but also wants to enter a convent and become a nun. When she chooses the celibate life of a nun, she limits herself—she can no longer marry.

A pastor must assist young couples who come to him for the purpose of discussing the advisability of marriage to determine whether the marriage is based on a sharing of mature love or not. Marriage is fraught with enough difficulty when based on mature love, but has little chance when based on hero worship or crush (romantic) love which often masquerades in our society as true love. A pastor, then, must help a couple to explore and determine if their desire to marry is based upon mature love, hero worship, or crush love.

In hero worship the individual gains a feeling of love-thrill when someone who has the adulation of other people shows special interest in him or her. Typically, the individual will not even know his or her hero in any real sense. The feeling of love-thrill derives not from meaningful interpersonal sharing, but is a feeling of ecstasy derived from the notion that he or she possesses someone that many other people want and don't have in this special way. In other words, the hero worshiper's ego needs are feeding on the public esteem achieved by the hero. (Often the young and handsome assistant pastor is the target of such hero worship and will understand this point well.)

For example, a young woman came to a minister and excitedly asked that plans be made for her church wedding. She said that she was planning to marry a popular rock-and-roll singer who, she admitted, she had not known very long. The pastor asked her to tell him something about the man. She answered: "Oh, he's just groovy—way far out—wait 'til you meet him; he's so handsome and popular with everyone. I know he likes me more than he does other girls because he always is giving me little presents and wants to marry me." After her conversation she left. The pastor later learned she had hastily married the singer in a civil ceremony. In a short time the marriage ended in divorce. Her "idol" was in reality a very self-centered, arrogant, thoughtless man with whom she could share nothing.

Similar problems are brought to the counselor by young adults who are caught up in the throes of crush love for each other. Each loves the idea of being loved by someone who, from the other's point of view, has many attractive characteristics. They are not, however, responding to each other as unique human beings but to the apparent feeling of love each has for the other. When plans—a little white cottage, two children, perhaps a dog—are thrown in, this is called "romance" or "romantic love." Romantic love, like hero worship, is not mature love, even though it is the major theme of romance magazines and most popular tunes of our day.

To illustrate, a young man and woman came to a clergyman to arrange their marriage. When counseling them, he noticed how romantic and affectionate they were toward each other as they held hands and discussed the marriage plans with him. The counselor found it difficult, however, to get them to talk about the realities of married life or to look at each other's personal qualities realistically. For example, they described the lovely little cottage they planned to have, but they had no idea how they were going to pay for it. Further, when the woman talked about her fiancé it seemed as if she were discussing some type of ideal man rather than the one who was sitting there. She would say things like, "Oh, I know he doesn't like to work now and would rather go fishing, but that will all change when we get married." His attitude toward her was no more realistic. He admitted that he noticed when he visited her apartment that the bed was unmade and dirty dishes were always in the sink. He assured the counselor that everything would change after marriage: "I am sure that Helen's apartment looks like it does because she has to live alone. I'm sure she'll be the model housewife after we get married." The counselor assumed that they were not looking at each other or accepting each other realistically and that they were basing their relationship upon the mutual thrill of being loved.

But they were married anyway. Soon after their honeymoon the feeling of thrill from being loved wore off and they discovered they could only regain the thrill by making up following fights—assuring each other of their love in dramatic ways. Once this discovery was made, the fights continued in earnest, including dish throwing by her and cursing and yelling by him. Neither could stop playing the crush game and avoid the tension it created. Finally, the tension became unbearable and the marriage ended in divorce.

Unlike the two cases cited above, it was a pleasure for a pastor many years ago to discuss marriage with a couple who shared mature love—they accepted and respected each other as they really were, including both their good and less fortunate qualities.

She was a nurse and he was a young doctor. It was good to hear her say to the counselor: "I'm not perfect but I know that Tom knows my weaknesses and loves me anyway. I will try to become the best wife and mother I can." Tom showed his maturity in the relationship by saying, "While I'm starting my practice, I won't be able to make enough money to give Martha the things I would like for her to have, but I'm sure she understands and is willing to make the sacrifices we both must make to build our lives together." Then he added this important remark: "She understands me better than anyone I've ever known and loves me in spite of it. And while she may not be the most beautiful woman in the world, she's all I want. She's the girl for me."

The nurse and doctor were married. Early in life, they had many personal as well as financial problems to bear. Two years after marriage the doctor had to have one of his lungs removed; their first baby was still-born shortly thereafter. Neither these or other problems or disappointments were sufficient to disrupt the marriage itself. The key to their success in large part was their unwavering love, which did not demand perfection from the other but involved acceptance, respect, and love of each for the other just as he or she was.

Conclusion

There are many professional counseling functions regarding the young adult that the pastor will be called upon to perform. Only a few have been enumerated and discussed here. The most important single function of the pastoral counselor is to assist the young adult to define, and perhaps at times redefine, his personal value system including moral and spiritual values.

Discussed also were the roles the counselor may play when a young adult comes to him about his occupational choices, his interpersonal relations—including the possibility and desirability of marriage—his need for self-esteem and encouragement, and his needs to overcome feelings of loneliness. The need for a mature and adequate value system is antecedent to all his other needs—for his occupational choice, his choice of friends and companions, his use of free time, his needs for encouragement, and so forth.

The pastor, then, has the duty to assist the young adult not only in developing a value system but also to assist him to determine goals and objectives within that value system which are consistent with his developing religious, moral, spiritual, and personal values.

7

MIDDLESCENCE

Understanding Middlescence

More and more it is being recognized that middle age, or "middlescence," as it is now called, is a distinct phase of human maturation and development with specific characteristics and unique problems and needs. The period of middlescence is a long one and the nature of the problems change according to the adjustments made earlier in this stage of development. Several characteristics of middlescence are important for the pastoral counselor to understand. Only three important ones will be considered: (1) critical changes in physical, mental, and emotional growth patterns; (2) fundamental reassessments of values, goals, objectives, and even vocations; and (3) concern about time and changing time perception.

1. Middlescence is a period of revolutionary changes, like the changes in adolescence, which challenge an individual's previous developmental adjustment and force him to alter his earlier values, goals, and objectives or to drop them and substitute new ones. The average professional football player reaching thirty-five does not have the physical stamina or acuity to continue playing the game as he did in the past and must change his profession and complete lifestyle.

Changes in physical growth patterns in middlescence are more obvious than changes in mental and emotional patterns. Menarche signaled a fundamental change in the adolescent girl's growth pattern; menopause delineates an equally significant change in the physical growth pattern of the middlescent woman. The changing sexuality in the male is less obvious than it was in adolescence: nevertheless, waning sexuality is equally as profound for him as the intense sexual drives that began in adolescence. These changes are both fundamental and traumatic for many people; the problems that these changes cause challenge the skill of the pastoral counselor.

A woman who had made her living as a professional model came to a pastoral counselor and hystcrically cried: "What am I going to do? My husband has run away with a sixteen-year-old girl and I don't know how to make a living except by modeling. I've done everything I know to keep my appearance but ever since menopause, I haven't been able to control my weight and keep my figure as I used to, and my hair is getting coarser by the month. I've even had my face lifted but the crows' feet keep showing up"—then a long pause— "I'm absolutely panicked. What on earth shall I do?" It was imperative that the pastor help the woman feel that all of her life was not over because of her age and that she was merely entering a new phase of life and would have to adjust her goals, objectives, and possibly find a new vocation.

2. The middlescent is going through a crisis in his life. He stands at a new crossroad. He looks back and evaluates his achievements and his interpersonal relationships. He reassesses his values, goals, and objectives on the bases of what he has gained and what he has paid psychologically and then determines whether or not he wants to buy for his future what he has bought with these values in the past. He feels the urgency of such decisions, because ordinarily a middlescent feels this is the one last chance to make a significant change in life-style that may lead to rewarding achievements and relationships with people which will be deeper and more satisfying. Sometimes he makes decisions recklessly at this time. It is the pastor's duty to assist a client not only to find more satisfying ways to live but also to help prevent him from making impetuous and sometimes tragic changes because he has failed to achieve what he had hoped he would or failed to form relationships which he wanted with others.

The counselor cannot prevent changes from occurring, but he can help a middlescent reassess and change his values in a mentally healthy way. For example, a client should not be encouraged to drop old values as if they had been mistakes with which he had wasted half his adult life. Instead, he should help the client find the inherent value in his earlier position to himself and others, while at the same time recognizing that he now wants something different for his future which is not necessarily morally better.

In many cases the middlescent changes her or his life-style completely. To illustrate, a woman who had been a nun in a convent for twenty years came to a counselor to discuss her desire for marriage and her own home. After counseling and with the permission of her church superiors, she left the convent and married. She then looked forward to her own home and raising the two children she and her husband were going to adopt. Again, a Roman Catholic priest who had left his religious community came to the same counselor for help in facing the critical crises that going out into the world had caused him, since he had never had to make a living before in his life. Or again, without success, a pastor tried to dissuade a woman, who decided she wanted to be an artist, from leaving her husband and going off with a younger painter.

Not long after, the counselor sought to help a middlescent couple whose children were grown and had left home. The man had been a respected college professor for years and she a high school teacher. Now they had decided that he would quit and sell real estate and she would open an antique shop. The consequences of such changes in life-styles caused both the man and woman to become anxious. They sought the help of the counselor. Up to now, their life-styles had been predicated primarily on intellectual values. Now they looked back and discovered that intellectual values alone would not meet the needs which now were felt to be paramount. The man wished to relate with people not as a parent to a child as he had done as a professor to his students but as an adult to other adults. She, in turn, felt that art appreciation was more satisfying than constant discipline problems in a schoolroom. The counselor assisted them in exploring the potential of each personality to make sure that such changes were consonant with their individual capabilities and consistent with their revised value systems.

There are many ways in which the pastoral counselor can assist middlescent men and women as they assess and reassess their value systems in terms of achievement and interpersonal relations. The following illustrations indicate a few ways in which the pastoral counselor can be helpful.

Several opportunities for individual counseling resulted from a group discussion between a minister and a dozen or so middlescent men. The discussion focused on the need for self-esteem and the esteem of others. It was concluded that in large part such esteem depended on one's feeling of achievement and the recognition by others of this achievement. Each man then asked himself two questions: What have I achieved—what tracks have I left? And what did it cost me or others? Several men felt satisfied that they had worked hard all their lives and had, along with a wife, raised children who were happily married and successful in life. They now looked forward to joyful visits with grandchildren. They anticipated a great deal of happiness by vicariously living exciting and happy lives through their grandchildren.

One man, a contractor, described with justifiable pride the church he had built which would serve as a monument to his creative ability and talent and would continue to be an active and useful structure in which he could continue to take pride as he grew older. Another man did not begrudge the time he had spent in scientific research for he would be known and respected for the rest of his life for his contributions to cancer research. Two other men remained silent; later each made an appointment with the pastor for personal counseling.

One of the men, John, came to the parsonage for counseling. He was the son of a very wealthy man and woman. He was now forty-five and had done nothing in his life but be a playboy. As he looked back, he realized he had accomplished nothing although he had spent a great deal of money on himself. The pastor counseling him found that although he was childless he had a great love for children. The pastor was aware of the need for personal and financial assistance at the city orphanage. John enthusiastically embraced the idea of becoming a member of the board of directors and taking an active part in helping the children. Two years after counseling he came back and said to the pastor: "Life never had any meaning for me before; now I can't wait to be with the children and see the happy looks on their faces when I simply pay attention to them. I'm also happy about the recreational building I helped design and am paying to have built. What a sense of satisfaction I will have, even when I'm old, knowing it will still make hundreds of children happy."

The other man from the group, Tom, who came for counseling had quite a different problem involving past achievements and the future. He was a very successful middlescent businessman and wealthy banker. Although he was not liked too well by people in the community, principally because he was ruthless with individuals who did not pay their notes on time, he was nevertheless respected as a businessman. The pastor was surprised that he came for counseling.

The counseling session began with a long awkward silence. Finally Tom spoke: "I don't know how to tell you about this . . . but . . . ever since our group discussion about self-esteem and achievement, I've been suffering the tortures of the damned." He paused and then continued: "You see, parson, as you know I'm a wealthy man. Well, I haven't been exactly dishonest in making money . . . I've always stayed within the law . . . but . . . but . . . I've driven some hard bargains in my day and lost the friendship of a lot of people. I haven't done anything crooked exactly, but I've stretched my conscience to get what I wanted. For example, it wasn't illegal for me to borrow some of the bank's funds, but I never payed the same interest on the money I borrowed which I demanded from customers." He sat for a long time, then said: "I'm miserable and unhappy; I've paid too much in self-respect and self-esteem for what I've got. I'm lonely and don't have people, importantly, in my life. What can I do, parson, about it?"

It was the pastor's role to help the man develop an adequate moral and spiritual value system and to find ways for him to alleviate his feelings of regret for his past life. The latter was accomplished by praying together that God would forgive the man any injustice he might have done his fellow man and anything that might have been dishonest. The problem of developing a value system necessitated more counseling sessions which included helping the client form a certain conscience in many moral matters. As a final result of the counseling, Tom chose new goals as a banker which incorporated the objective to do all that he could to help new young couples and homeless people find suitable and reasonable housing. As a banker he was in a unique position to know when reasonable housing was available because he dealt regularly with all the real estate agencies in the city. In the years that followed, Tom was successful in helping many people; he became a well-liked citizen in the community, and, of great importance to him, he developed many close and rewarding friendships.

Opportunities for counseling a group of middlescent women regarding interpersonal relationships resulted from another group discussion in which the woman's group in the church were discussing what they considered necessary for self-fulfillment and personal happiness. The questions they asked themselves were similar to those the men asked regarding past achievements. They asked two questions also: Have my interpersonal relationships been satisfactory in the past? Have my goals been sufficiently rewarding that I want to carry them into the future?

Most of the women concluded that they would not wish to change their interpersonal relationships. They were all happily married, loved their husbands and their children, and had satisfactory and rewarding friendships with men and women with whom they associated. It was clear, however, that the discussion was painful for three of the women. Each came subsequently to the pastor for counseling. Each case illustrates a different facet of problems that arises from unsatisfactory interpersonal relationships.

The first woman to come to the pastor was a fifty-one-year-old woman who had been married four times, divorced three times, and now was considering divorcing her fourth husband. She opened the counseling session by saying: "I really feel down in the dumps. I've had the darndest luck in marriage and I don't know why. My first husband and I were married when we were both nineteen, after we had been sleeping together for a year, because we were afraid I had gotten pregnant. Wouldn't you know he ran away with another woman? I divorced him when I learned they had a baby . . . And then my second husband. I met him at a dance and thought what a handsome and wonderful man he was. I knew him only a week and we got married. Three months after we got married he came home with a serious and contagious disease [she meant a venereal disease]. Also during our short marriage he turned out to be a thoughtless and cruel person. I divorced him after only three and one-half months of marriage.

"I really thought I had it made with my third husband. He was a rich man who spoiled me with all sorts of presents before we got married. It wasn't long after we married that I realized I'd made a mistake. He was twenty years older than me and we didn't have anything in common. For example, I liked to go to dances but he would say that at his age he hadn't the energy to dance. After our relationship reached a complete standoff, I divorced him.

"After about two months I met my present husband at a dance. He waited on me hand and foot before we got married, but wouldn't you know, as soon as we got married, he began complaining constantly about his aches and pains. In addition, because he considered himself a sick man, he expected me to wait on him all the time . . . I've sure made a mess of things, haven't I?"

The counselor had to agree. He knew that her early values and subsequent goals led her to focus entirely on her own needs and wants in any relationship. Further, he knew that to obtain and maintain the relationships she really wanted in her future, she would have to buy them by showing interest in the basic needs and wants of other people with whom she wished to share rewarding interpersonal relationships. During the counseling sessions he was able to show the woman that her own immature self-interest was the cause of much of her earlier problems and her resulting inability to share mutual and mature love with others.

After several counseling sessions, the pastor called in both the woman and her husband and he was able to assist the couple in understanding her problem. About a year after counseling, the woman returned. She said: "You know, I've had things all wrong for a long time. I never really knew what love was until you helped me look at my problems as they actually existed and helped me to learn to love in an altruistic way. Would you believe it, his sicknesses don't bother me any more—and he really does have some serious health problems—I kinda enjoy taking care of him, for when I do, he's so grateful it makes me feel all warm inside. I didn't realize, either, how much he loved me until I changed my attitude toward him—

now, he's always trying to find little things to please me like buying me that pretty little dress I didn't know he knew I wanted."

The second woman, Helen, had a genuine problem which she had not created but which involved interpersonal relationships. Helen had had four children. Her only daughter died when she was three years old, her youngest boy at six years, and her two oldest sons were killed in an airplane crash when they were twenty-three and twenty-five respectively. She came to see the pastor soon after the crash when she learned that her husband was dying of a heart condition. She was unhappy not only because her children were dead but also because, as she looked back now, she had left no tracks —the children she had expected to be her tracks were gone. Soon, too, she would need help to face the lonely days when her husband died.

Such a person often ends up in depression and despair. Fortunately, as a part of her moral and spiritual value system, the woman had great faith in God, in her Church, and she believed in life with God and loved ones after death. She did not change her value system but reinforced her earlier beliefs. The pastor spent a good deal of time in assisting the woman to readjust her life within her value system. After the husband's death, as she had been advised, she became more and more active in church societies and activities. Such activities not only made her feel needed but also provided her with many valued interpersonal relationships with other members of the church.

The third woman who came to the pastor for counseling was one who was a recent convert to Catholicism. She was a single woman of forty-four. She was well-dressed and very nice-looking. After a few moments she began: "I'm so ashamed of myself I had to come to talk to you after that meeting, when we talked about self-fulfillment and personal happiness and our relationships with other people. I can't sleep at night any more after that discussion. I've got to have some help about changing my ways because I'm lonely most of the time, and, also, I don't respect myself and the way I live." She paused, then continued: "I hope it won't shock you but I'm a kept woman. I've known a man for many years. He's married and has children. He has money and travels a great deal on business. He doesn't live here, but he pays the rent on my apartment, gives me an allowance, and stays with me when he's in town which is about once a week." She paused again and tearfully, continued: "It just isn't worth it. He's the only person in my life and when I look at our relationship, it is only a superficial one. I'm just his sex object and nothing more. I've got to do something. Please help me."

As in many other cases, it was necessary for the counselor to assist the woman in developing a new moral and spiritual value system and to help her thereby to regain her self-respect and self-esteem. The genuine and honest respect the counselor showed the woman regardless of her behavior was supportive as she gradually learned to respect herself. A short time after the first counseling session, she broke with the man she had been living with, got a job, and began a new life. Two years later she met a widower with two grown children and they were married. The counselor was pleased to hear her say one day: "I didn't know life could be so rich and beautiful. Some say life begins at forty; mine began at forty-six. Not only do I have a deep and intense relationship with Ralph, but also together we have many warm friendships with other couples our age."

3. Time becomes a major concern for the middlescent. As his metabolism slows down, his perception of time speeds up. Even though he does not want to do so, he must accept the fact that time is running out and that at least half of his life is gone. Much of the impatience shown by the middlescent stems from his great uncertainty about the time remaining. Time can, in many cases, become an obsession and this can lead to a maladaptive use of the time he has left.

For example, a well-to-do and successful doctor came to a pastor to complain about the inability his family had in understanding his behavior, which they said was disrupting family life and causing arguments and disagreements. He said: "Can't they see that I'm fifty-five years old and that if I don't work extra hard, I can't pay off the place in the country before I retire five years from now." As he continued, the counselor learned that in addition to his heavy duties in a hospital, he disrupted his family's life by taking private patients at his home early each morning before he went to the hospital and then saw patients each evening after supper and still others on Saturdays. The counselor suggested that he might be paying too big a price both physically and in terms of his family life for his place in the country. In his case, however, he did not choose to change his intense focus on time or substitute more humanly gratifying goals. Six months after seeing the pastor, the doctor was found dead in bed of a heart attack from overwork.

Another example of concern for time, past achievements, and future goals is the typical middlescent's pastime of following the career achievements of his college classmates in an alumni magazine. He is quick to compare his achievements with theirs, feeling elated when he discovers that he is in a higher position than they are and disconcerted, even depressed, when he finds his achievements in no way match theirs. Characteristically, too, one often finds the middlescent scrutinizing the obituary notices in his professional magazines and feeling encouraged when he finds his colleagues are dying at relatively old ages but feeling distressed when he notices a younger one has died.

To repeat, concerns with time, with changing growth patterns, and with values, goals, objectives, life-styles, and vocations are characteristic of the middlescent. There are many others but those discussed are particularly important for the pastoral counselor to understand.

Special Problems of Middlescence

Just as there are many physical and emotional characteristics unique to middlescence, there are certain special needs and problems found in middlescence. Some of the more important problems are (1) identity problems; (2) specific problems related to friendship and love at this time of life; and (3) problems which may develop because of morbid fixation and fear of physical deterioration and may arise as middlescence ends and a person must face the reality of old age and death.

1. *Identity problems* are almost as common in middlescence as in adolescence. A good rule of thumb is that good adjustments during the major growth periods earlier in life are predictive of easier adjustments during subsequent growth periods; conversely, poor adjust-

ments earlier in life will make subsequent adjustments harder. As it was demonstrated when discussing the characteristics of this phase of life, the middlescent may become disappointed and discouraged because he has left no tracks—he has yet to build a monument to show he has lived—or because his idealistic goals and aspirations as a young man were unrealistic and he must now settle for less—abandon his goals or substitute new ones for the short time he feels remains.

The identity problem is, typically, aggravated by waning idealism and increasing cynicism regarding religious, civic, political, and similar values. The pastoral counselor will be called upon to assist clients not only to overcome disappointment and discouragement because goals have not been met but also to work through the disillusionment and cynicism that may develop regarding values in general, and specifically moral and religious values. The approaches recommended for the pastoral counselor are exemplified in the following cases:

A fifty-year-old doctor came for counseling because he felt discouraged and disappointed with himself. As he said: "I really haven't accomplished anything meaningful to me in life. Now I'm no longer interested in trying and, besides, I don't have the energy I used to have. When I was a young doctor, I promised myself that I would not only give good care to my patients but also would spend my spare time in working on improved hospital conditions and care for the patients. Somehow, I never got around to the proposed project. The years slipped by. I got married. I had a busy practice. Now I don't have the physical or psychic energy, nor, I'm ashamed to say, the interest or desire to pursue my early ambitions. Often, though, I feel I've done nothing really important in my life and I've never really achieved my potential as a real person."

Helping the doctor overcome his feelings of discouragement for failing to achieve his earlier goals was the counselor's first task. Helping the doctor see and appreciate, personally, the good he had done by his devotion to his medical profession, by the care he had given his patients, and by the lives he had saved helped him overcome his feeling of discouragement and that his past life was a total waste.

Next the counselor impressed upon the doctor that while his

idealism had waned, a significant ideal still remained, namely, to achieve according to his talents, which the pastor knew to be exceptional. He recommended that the doctor explore possible areas or activities which would make the realization of this ideal possible. In this case, the doctor and his wife joined the Peace Corps and set up a hospital in southern Chile. The doctor found life intensely rewarding as he trained new medical personnel in his own hospital.

Dealing with a forty-seven-year-old contractor, Carl, took somewhat longer. In the initial counseling session Carl stated: "I came to you because I feel down in the dumps so much of the time and can't seem to shake it. Everything seems blah to me. I don't give a damn about anything; life itself is a pain. I've got no ambition to do anything. It was a lot different when I was young. Then I dreamed of designing and constructing a spacious, beautiful home which everyone would see and admire me for my talent and ability. Somewhere along the line I lost my oomph. Now, frankly, I only do contracting for the money that's in it. I don't really care what I build or how sloppy and junky it is."

In the first session the counselor helped Carl see that his lethargy and disgust with himself was caused by the absence of any rewarding achievements in the past or satisfying goals or objectives in the future. It was suggested by the counselor that the client explore and set new goals within his current interests. Surprisingly, he showed interest in dealing with people rather than things. He continued in the contracting business in order to make a living, but he became an enthusiastic consulter and director of a local little league baseball association. He found this a new rewarding way to live. Within three years the pastor found that Carl was building an unusual and functionally creative youth center which he designed and which was being financed by every major men's club in town.

Cases which involve cynicism and disillusionment about civic, political, and religious values are brought regularly to a pastoral counselor as the following two illustrations indicate.

Henry came to the pastor for counseling at the request of his wife. He began: "I didn't want to come here but Sally said she was going to leave me if I didn't go see someone and get some help." When asked what kind of help he needed, Henry replied: "Sally says we can't even have company anymore because, as she says, I'm always going on and on complaining about the no-good people we have in government and of bad politicians in particular. She's so pollyanna-ish about every one, it makes me sick. Most people are rotten to the core and she can't see it."

In order to understand the cause for Henry's cynicism, the pastor had Henry tell him about his earlier life. Henry was now fifty-one. The counselor learned that he had served with distinction in World War II. He came home with great civic and political ideals. He decided to fulfill these ideals by entering political life as a means of serving his country and fulfilling himself. Eventually, he was elected to the House of Representatives of his state. This was ten years before Henry came for counseling. During those years, Henry became increasingly disillusioned about the operation of the bureaucratic state government and became cynical about his fellow repre-sentatives after he learned that many of them were involved in dis-honest schemes while proclaiming, hypocritically, their loyalty to the system and their genuine interest and concern for their constituents.

The counselor began by helping his reluctant client understand that it isn't rules or ideals which are bad but how people use or abuse them. In addition, he was able to help Henry see that pre-cisely because some do not honor political values, it was important for men like Henry to fight even harder to see that they become effective and were not completely destroyed.

Subsequently, Henry discovered that his inside knowledge of the politicians and their abuse of the political process in the state was of inestimable value to the state's prosecuting attorney. At Henry's sug-gestion, the attorney looked into the corruption in the state politics and prosecuted, successfully, the offenders. Henry ran for office again and won. He found when he returned to the legislature that being a politician in a politically cleaned-up state was very reward-ing. He overcame his cynicism and regained much of his older politi-cal idealism.

An important case which involved cynicism and disillusionment regarding moral and spiritual ideals was brought to a pastor by a forty-three-year-old woman. He knew her to be a faithful and devout member of the congregation. She stated that she had enjoyed her church and she had a faith she thought could not be shaken, but a short time before she came for counseling, she had found she was mistaken.

She related the following: "I was so happy with my church and my faith until four months ago when I quit my job downtown and was able, for the first time, to join our ladies auxiliary. What a shock I got at the first meeting I attended! I believed that every professed Christian practiced the commandments of the Lord, especially, 'You shall love your neighbor as yourself.' I found out it wasn't true. After the regular meeting, while we were having refreshments, I was shocked to hear one of the ladies I thought was such a good Christian say: 'Did you hear the latest about our new assistant—well, I got it on good authority that although he is married, he has been going out with a young lady—I don't dare say her name—but you know whom I mean—she plays the organ at the nine o'clock Sunday service.' All the ladies got quiet. I started to say that I thought it was awful they were talking that way when another of the ladies spoke up quickly and said: 'You know I'm not surprised. I noticed several times how they smiled at each other in a knowing way when she began to play for a service.' Before I could say anything another of the ladies said: 'He looks like the kind of man who would—well, you know what I mean.' This went on until I could stand it no longer; I went home and cried. I was stunned to discover that in my church that kind of vicious backbiting went on by fellow Christians. I have been even more disturbed when it came out that what they were saying was true. Frankly, I don't think I have any faith left; sometimes I doubt if I ever did have any real faith."

It was clear that not only was her faith shaken as regards her fellow Christians, but also that she was questioning the validity of her faith in God and Christian spiritual values and ideals. Christianity was, to all appearances in her mind, a failure because it did not effect changes in the destructive and immoral behavior of the members of the church.

The pastor at the outset assured her that he understood the pain and confusion she was experiencing and that he, too, found it unfortunate when Christians failed to live up to their faith. He reminded her, however, that there was only one Christ who was perfect and that human beings, including Christians, do not always live up perfectly to moral standards and rules because they are free to ignore or violate ethical and moral codes of behavior. As a practical remedy, he suggested that she not give up her faith but strengthen it by using prayer to include petitions for the women, who, in her eyes, were violating the moral commandment of God, that they might become more charitable and loving of others and prayers for the well-being of the minister and the woman accused of immoral behavior with him. She promised to do so and return a week later.

When she returned she asked the pastor to assist her to a mature faith which she realized she never had. Tearfully, she admitted that her religious faith in the past had been operating upon youthful idealism alone and that in retrospect she could see her religion was just form and formality and had generated no relevance for her practical everyday living. Now, when it seemed apparently useless in one area, she found that she had never made real use of it in any meaningful aspect of her entire life. When it seemed to fail in one area, she was ready to discard faith completely.

The pastor not only gave her instructions to help her develop a mature faith but also helped her find realistic ways that she could use to make spiritual values more relevant to her life. He helped her find, among other things, a specific way that she could actively witness her faith and practice fraternal charity. He asked her to be the chairwoman for the annual drive for clothing for the city's needy and then to distribute the clothing personally. She readily accepted and found that although it was hard work, it was also a rewarding and fulfilling experience which strengthened her faith and renewed her spiritual and moral value system.

2. *Problems related to friendship and love* are a second major source of difficulty for the middlescent. Certain of these problems have been alluded to and discussed earlier. However, there are certain specific problems in this area which warrant further consideration. Three of these are (a) problems due to changing sexuality, (b) problems due to readjustments in interpersonal relationships that may be necessary, and (c) problems due to difficulties in establishing new and meaning relationships at this age.

a. Changing sexuality is a deep concern to the middlescent. The fear that he cannot perform sexually and adequately haunts many middle-aged men and may spur them on to increased sexual activities to prove their continued virility.

For example, a middlescent man came to a pastor for counseling. Because he discovered that it now took a more sexually stimulating object to gain tumescence, he had broken off a relationship with an older woman and married a girl of nineteen. Soon after marriage, he began to fear he could not satisfy her sexually because of his advancing age. Unfortunately, as he explained to the counselor, the more he worried about it, the less able he was to perform. When he came for counseling he was relatively impotent. He was discouraged and disheartened. The counselor assured him that he had been informed by doctors that many men can perform adequately even into old age. He referred the client to a psychologist for help in overcoming his fears, which, in all probability, were the cause for his impotency.

A more difficult problem was presented to a pastor by a woman from his congregation. Tearfully she related: "I don't know what has come over my husband. I always thought he was faithful to me and that I satisfied him sexually. Now after twenty-two years of marriage, he is carrying on an affair with a woman who is young enough to be his daughter. I know it's going on because he comes home and brags about what a lady-killer he is and how young ladies, such as the one he is seeing, go for an older experienced man like himself. I think the old goat is simply making a fool of himself, but it hurts just the same to see him do it."

The counselor handled the case in a two-fold manner. First he assured the wife that, unfortunate as it was, it did happen that middlescent men sometimes, feeling their waning sexuality, seek out younger women with whom they have relations or who, at least, make them feel that they are sexually adequate and exciting. Next, the counselor, with the wife's permission, discussed the matter with her husband. During the counseling session the counselor was able to help the man to see not only what he was really doing, namely, unnecessarily attempting to assure himself of his masculinity, but also the potential consequences to his marriage if he continued. When the counselor finished, the man sheepishly remarked: "I guess the old saying's right—'there's no fool, like an old fool.' I get your point, pastor; I'll take care of the matter." The counselor assisted the man in his resolution to handle the matter adaptively by assisting him to see the relatively greater value to himself of a deep, mature relationship with his wife and family rather than the value of ongoing sexual prowess.

b. Readjustment in interpersonal relationships poses one of the most serious problems for many middlescent men and women, particularly for married couples. In middlescence, after twenty or twenty-five years of marriage, the children have left home and a couple must re-evaluate their interpersonal relationship and may need to find new ways and means to improve the love shared between them.

To illustrate, a man and wife after twenty-two years of marriage came to see a counselor shortly after their youngest daughter had left home to get married. According to the couple, they came to the counselor as a last resort before obtaining a divorce. She began: "It may surprise you that Percy and I have come to see you after being married so many years, but we are thinking about getting a divorce. You see, except for the children, we don't have much in common. He likes sports and he drives me crazy spending all his spare time watching football games on TV. Also, he's begun drinking too much and gets grouchier every time he drinks. Also, I hate living out in the country like we do; I'd like to be in a city where I can see more people, go to a movie, and get away from him and the house."

When he discussed his wife privately with the counselor, Percy stated: "Theresa is all right I guess. She took good care of the kids and she's a good cook, but we just don't seem to have anything to talk about. She buys all those women's magazines that are supposed to tell about true romances but seem to me to be a lot of sentimental junk. She, still at her age, spends hours primping herself in front of a mirror. She keeps trying to look glamorous, like young movie stars she likes so much. Besides, I like the quiet of the country more and more, but she wants to be running around all the time in town. She'd wear any man out."

Similar statements were forthcoming from the man and woman during subsequent counseling sessions, clearly showing that except for the children, apparently, they had shared very little during their marriage and no deep interpersonal love. In order to help the clients, it was necessary at the beginning of counseling to determine if the couple honestly wanted and were willing to work at establishing a mature love relationship and to determine whether they felt they had enough in common to make such an effort worthwhile. The counselor discovered that they really did wish to continue living together because each feared loneliness and the inability to find another partner at their age. This was not a great deal to start with, but it did give impetus to attempts to find ways for them to share the kind of love each wanted.

After working with them for some time, the counselor found that although some highly visible interests were not shared in common, there were many subtle and beautiful things that they had shared for years without realizing it, which they could continue to share for the rest of their lives. Their common religious faith and similar moral and spiritual values were among the most important things they had taken for granted all these years. The counselor helped them build their mutual love on these and other beautiful and meaningful things they had shared. During the counseling process he also helped them find new interests which they could share and that would contribute to an ever-deepening interpersonal relationship.

c. One of the most difficult problems for a middlescent is how to form new and deep interpersonal love relationships. In some cases this is due to the inability to adapt to new relationships because of past experiences, because of expectations that certain elements must be present in a new relationship which were present in a satisfying earlier one, and because of a general personal rigidity which is characteristic of middlescence.

For example, Paul had been married for twenty-five years. His wife had been an excellent homemaker, cook, and mother. The parents of both Paul and his wife had come from the same European country, and therefore the two shared many cultural and racial interests as well as a deep, mature love. Unfortunately, the woman developed cancer and died.

Paul remained a widower approximately a year. After that, he obeyed his dying wife's admonition that she did not want him to remain alone and wanted him to marry again—he married Marie, a woman whom both his deceased wife and he had known for twenty years. In fact, she worked as a business secretary in Paul's office and had been a constant companion of Paul's wife before her death. However, unlike Paul's first wife, Marie had lived as a spinster all her forty-three years and knew little about homemaking since she had worked in an office all her adult life. Too, she had a different ethnic background from Paul and his first wife.

Paul came to the counselor dejected and disheartened. He explained: "This is nothing like the wonderful marriage I had with Elsa. I don't know what to do about it. Marie is a fine woman but I don't think we can make it. I know we can't without help." With the permission of Paul, the counselor called both Paul and Marie to his office. He was able to help them see that human beings can share mature love with more than one person but it may be in completely different ways. He helped Paul to see that he should not expect Marie to be a replica and continuation of Elsa. He further helped Paul to understand that Marie, who had lived alone all her adult life, had as many or more adjustments to make in adapting her living style to take into account the wants, needs, and even the presence of another person in her home.

Starting with these premises, it was possible for the counselor to assist the couple to a mature, shared love uniquely different from that which Paul and his first wife had enjoyed. Seventeen years later, Paul and Marie in their old age still shared a beautiful relationship, different but equally deep and meaningful as the love Paul and Elsa had shared earlier.

3. A third group of problems may develop because of morbid fixations and fears about physical deterioration. These usually arise as middlescence ends and one must face the reality of old age and death. Certain kinds of physical deterioration do, indeed, accelerate at this time and the counselor must assist a client to face them.

Many middlescents cannot or refuse to face the reality of impending old age, which must end in death. This was illustrated, tragically, in two cases carried in the public press. One story told of a famous actress who became morbidly obsessed about her physical condition and deterioration. She began to take more and more tranquilizers and sleeping pills. She finally took an overdose and was found dead in her bed. The other story carried in the press was that of a prominent fifty-six-year-old rich socialite who committed suicide by jumping from the window of her New York apartment. The note

she left stated: "I am going to 'end it all. I can't face growing old
and unattractive. I'd rather end it now."

In all cases brought to the pastoral counselor which involve physical debility and fear of old age, he should encourage the client to
live fully in the present although realistically planning for the future. He must help the client redefine his moral and spiritual values
so that they will dispel the gloom and feelings of despair that could
arise for one approaching old age and death. The following case illustrates the technique used by a minister in counseling one woman.

The minister was called to the hospital because Shirley, one of his
parishioners, had attempted suicide by slashing her wrists. Fortunately, she was unsuccessful in her attempt. When he arrived, she
cried: "I don't want to live. I'm fifty-eight years old and alone in this
world. I never had a husband or, for that matter, a real close friend.
I can't stand the thought of being a lonely old woman with no one
to love and need me. I can't even have a respectable disease so that I
can die and get it over with. I'm just going to be an old, lonely
woman without anyone and a nuisance to my family." He let her
continue to talk. Finally, he asked her what she did professionally.
She replied: "Oh, I'm a psychiatric nurse. I work with a bunch of
delinquent kids down on Third Street; most of them have no families or don't know who their parents are." The counselor asked her if
she enjoyed her work. She answered: "Oh, yes. If it hadn't been for
it, I would have ended it a long time ago."

The fact remained that her work was not meeting her basic needs
and the counselor discovered she had no goals outside her work. He
helped her explore her interests and potential goals. To the surprise
of both client and counselor, she discovered an interest in learning to
square dance in the After-Forty-Club. In addition, to her amazement
she looked forward to Wednesday evenings when she met with a
group of neighborhood women who were quilting for a local orphanage. To the counselor's final surprise, he discovered that she was taking a course in ceramics in the local county adult education program
and was making him a set of dishes. Clearly, she was too busy and
happy to consider suicide.

Conclusion

Middlescence has been shown to be an important and significant phase of human maturation and development. To counsel the middlescent effectively and efficiently is a challenge to the pastoral counselor because of the variety and complexity of things that can become problems in this phase of human existence. The counselor must understand the profound effect that changes in physical, mental, and emotional growth patterns have upon the middlescent. He must be available, when asked, to assist the middlescent reassess or redefine his moral and spiritual values and help him determine realistic goals, objectives which will be rewarding for the rest of his life. He must understand the middlescent's preoccupation with time and his changing time perception. He must assist the middlescent to plan and use his remaining time in a rewarding manner.

The counselor must be prepared to help the middlescent with problems which involve identity crises, problems related to interpersonal relations, and problems that must be faced because of physical deterioration, impending old age, and death.

The counselor must be particularly prepared to help a client overcome discouragement, disillusionment, cynicism, and despair which may arise because of these problems. The moral and spiritual value system of a client becomes increasingly important to an individual in enabling him to overcome these negative feelings. It is essential that a pastor assist the middlescent to form or re-form his moral and spiritual value system so that a man or woman can withstand the stress, strain, and anxiety these feelings produce and will continue to generate.

8

THE ELDERLY

Understanding the Elderly

In the geriatric years the cycle of dependency and independency of a person is completed. As it has been shown, the infant begins life as a totally dependent being and slowly moves toward independence. Impetus for increasing independence is given in adolescence. Soon a person finds he cannot live totally alone. He then must adjust and constantly readjust his independence and mutual interdependence with others throughout his adult life. Finally, in old age, he moves to increasing dependence on others so that in some cases the debilitated or bedridden elderly man or woman becomes, as was the infant, totally dependent on others—dependent, often, on the very ones who in earlier life depended on him—his children.

To understand the elderly, the pastoral counselor must be aware of (1) the physical changes and changes in growth patterns of the aging and (2) the mental state and attitude—often rigid—of the elderly man or woman.

1. Profound physical changes take place in old age. Strength wanes as muscles begin to atrophy. Energy plays out quickly. Digestive problems begin to increase, sleep patterns change, eyesight dims, hearing losses occur, and physical changes in the brain and memory tracks are such that an elderly person may be able to recall what he did thirty years ago and cannot remember what he had for dinner

the day before. The counselor must understand the physical state of the elderly and often must counsel men and women who take care of an elderly patient or relative to help them understand how physical changes have affected the whole personality of the older person.

To illustrate, Mary came to the pastor for advice and counsel. She stated: "I don't know what to do; I'm about at my wits end . . . You see, Tom's mother, who is seventy, lives with us and has done so since she became a widow ten years ago. I had always liked her and agreed it would be fine for her to come live with us since all our children were grown and didn't live at home anymore. For several years everything seemed to be going well. We had a good time together. I enjoyed her as I would have enjoyed my own mother who died fifteen years ago. Later, however—I'd say for the last three years —things have changed. She's grouchy and up and down all night long. Even when we try to give her sleeping pills, she refuses to take them and she doesn't sleep all night long. Consequently, she cat-naps all day long and is irritated when some noise awakens her. I don't mind that so much, but what's getting me is she is constantly complaining about what I feed her—nothing seems to please her anymore. She used to like my cooking—or at least, she said so many times years ago—but now, even when I make her hot tamale pie that she liked so well when she first came to live with us, she won't eat. In fact, she has a whole list of things she won't eat now. I just don't seem to be able to please her at all. I don't know what to do—that's why I've come to talk to you. Oh yes, and another thing. I get so provoked at her because she can't seem to remember where she puts things. Several times a day I have to stop my work to help her find her glasses. I think this is ridiculous. She can remember and keeps reminding me of the time I dented the fender of our car eight years ago but she pretends she can't remember where she laid her glasses an hour before. I think she just wants me to wait on her."

The pastor hastened to assure the woman that he was not a doctor or an expert on geriatrics; however, he had been required to attend seminars conducted by doctors and others to help a counselor and those he counseled understand, in a general way, phenomena that were often characteristic of elderly persons. He could say to the woman: "Mary, I wouldn't be upset. I'm sure your mother-in-law still loves you but the aging process has changed her and not her

feelings for you. In fact, what you have described about her behavior
is considered normal for an elderly person. Take, for example, her
restlessness at night and cat-napping in the daytime. Doctors tell us
this is typical of older people. They cat-nap at night and have to cat-
nap in the daytime because they have had so little sleep at night.
Some doctors say it is a mistake to give such a person sleeping pills.
It is also a mistake for older people to expect to sleep like they did
when they were younger. Frequently interrupted nocturnal sleep
should be expected by elderly persons and should be supplemented
by naps in the daytime—just as it happens with a young baby.

"In the second place," the counselor continued, "many, if not
most, elderly people have or develop digestive problems as they lose
the digestive enzymes they had earlier. I've no doubt she enjoyed
your tamale pie ten years ago, but it is possible her digestive system
now can't take the hot sauce and chili peppers one ordinarily puts in
such a pie.

"Finally, I should say it is not ridiculous that she can remember
something that happened years ago and can't remember what she
did the day before or can't find something she laid down just a few
hours before. At one of the seminars I attended, although I didn't
understand all the technical sides of what a physiological psychologist was saying, I got the clear impression that it was normal, as a
part of the aging process of the brain, for short-term memory, as
remembering recent things was called, to become faulty before remote memory of things in the distant past were forgotten. In other
words, what I am trying to say is that it would seem that your
mother-in-law is acting normally for a woman of seventy. I wouldn't
worry about it, even though it means you and your husband must
adjust to her change in personality."

2. Often a pastor is asked to assist a man or woman in understanding the mental states and often rigid attitudes of an elderly
loved one. The case presented to a counselor by Philip is typical.

Philip came to the pastor to discuss the problems he was having
with his elderly father who was living in his home. He began: "I
love my father—God knows I do—but we just can't get along and I
don't know what to do about it. I've come to discuss the problem and
I want you to help me decide whether I can work it out so he can

stay with me and the wife and the kids or if I will have to put him in an old folks' home. I sure need help."

The counselor asked Philip to explain the problem as best he could. "As I see it," Philip said, "it's that Dad simply can't look at things as they are now—he's always living in the past—I can't get him to see that times have changed and you can't live today according to the—what do you call them—standards or rules that he made us live by as kids. I keep telling him he's gotta change. This is not 1925. But he doesn't see it and won't change.

"One of our biggest problems comes over my way of disciplining my kids. Dad believed, when we were young, the old saying, 'Spare the rod and spoil the child.' I considered it a great day when I got by without a spanking. Well, I don't believe in that kind of discipline for most things, especially for my son Carl. He's a very sensitive kid and gets his feelings hurt a lot. Spanking him when he does something he shouldn't doesn't seem to work, but if I lecture him and take away his privilege to watch TV, he comes around in a hurry. Dad argues that I'm not handling Carl the way I should . . . I don't think this can go on; either he's got to change or I'm probably gonna have to put him in a home. What do you think?"

The counselor replied: "Philip, you have the same problem that many others have in understanding and communicating with an elderly parent or loved one, but I don't think you'll have to put your father in a home to solve it. You see, not only is the past more real for your father but also, he has not much future to look forward to and therefore sees no reason for changing his values and standards. His standards and life-style worked for him in the past and he sees no reason to change for the short life left to him. You simply are not going to change this, Philip, but if you understand, you will be able to work out the problem of communication which exists between you and your father. You can come to respect each other's value system even if they are different. What I suggest, Philip, is that you and your father sit down and calmly talk over your different values and standards. And as I have counseled many others, each of you must try not only to respect the sincerity of the other but also understand and respect your differences. Why don't you and your father come to see me and perhaps I can help the two of you improve your

communication and understanding of each other and your differences."

Philip brought his elderly father with him a week later. One session with the counselor was sufficient to help them to begin to listen,
respectfully, to each other and to understand and communicate with
each other better. Philip saw the counselor at a football game some
months later. He stated: "You sure helped Dad and me—actually,
we're getting a kick out of comparing our different points of view
and comparing old times with today. Don't tell the old man, but I'm
learning a lot from him when he talks about how he was brought up
that'll help me with my own rules."

As indicated, one of the most valuable contributions a counselor
can make in such situations is to assist two generations to bridge the
gap that separates them. Rather than conflict, it can happen that
both generations will benefit by an open, respectful exchange of
ideas regarding values and differences without insisting that either
change his value system.

Problems of the Elderly

The problems of the elderly are many and varied. Five problem
areas are particularly important for the pastor to understand so that
he can counsel wisely. These arise for the aged because of (1) loss of
security, (2) fear of isolation, (3) feelings of uselessness, (4) fear of
unwanted dependency, and (5) the reality of impending death.

1. *Loss of security* presents many painful problems and causes
anxiety in elderly men and women. For example, a man and his
wife had a nice home. Shortly after retiring from his job, the man
died. The woman was now forced to live on a small pension. She
could no longer make the mortgage payments on her large house.
She had to sell the house and move into an apartment. She had
never lived in an apartment in all her life. She found it hard to adjust. When she had her home, she had friendly neighbors; in the
apartment no one even said hello. She had a nice flower garden
around her own home; now she lived on the eighth floor of a building
where she could not raise the flowers she loved.

She came to the counselor and sadly stated: "I've lost everything that has meant anything to me in my life. I felt so secure when Ted was alive and we had our own home. Now I feel like I am hopelessly drifting in a sea I don't understand—I've lost my roots and everything that is dear to me. What can I do? I don't want to go live with my married daughter. She's got enough on her hands with five children to raise. I don't want to go to an old folks' home. I would like to have some freedom and privacy of my own. I just don't know which way to turn."

After the counselor assured her that he understood her feelings, he asked her: "Do you happen to know Nellie Fox?" The woman answered: "Oh yes, she's a lovely woman. Years ago when her husband and mine were alive we used to meet at the country club." "Interestingly enough," the counselor continued, "she has a similar problem. Isn't it possible that the two of you might consider living together in the same apartment? Between you, I am sure you could afford one that would permit each of you to have your own room and privacy while sharing the rest of the apartment."

The woman's face lit up: "What a wonderful idea. I'll call her today. Do you have her phone number?" When the counselor said he did, she took the number and left. Two weeks later she and Nellie came to see him to announce that they thought living together was an excellent idea. They both seemed excited about it since they had so much in common. In fact, as one announced: "We've decided not to live in an apartment at all. We found a nice little cottage near a shopping center on the other side of town. The yard isn't large, but we both love flowers and we'll be able to have a tiny garden of our own." They lived together for eight years until Nellie died. By that time the other woman was a semi-invalid and asked to be placed in a home where her physical needs could be cared for.

2. *Fear of isolation* is a problem with some subtle similarities to the problem just discussed. The difference is that whereas the fear of insecurity derives from loss of familiar objects, such as a home, fear of isolation creates anxiety because of loss of important interpersonal relationships.

To illustrate, Martha, now seventy, came to the counselor and painfully stated: "I'm so lonely I don't know what to do. Horace, my husband, is dead and so are most of my old friends. I feel I'm all alone waiting for death. The world's passed me by. My children are grown and have moved away with their families. I just feel nobody needs me and, sometimes, that no one cares. I live alone and I keep thinking not only that nobody needs me but also what would happen if I fell and broke my hip and couldn't get to the telephone to call for help? What would I do? I'm haunted day and night that something will happen to me and I won't be able to get help. What shall I do?"

The counselor said to her: "Martha, first I would make it a point to have someone that knows you telephone you at least once a day when you are home to see if you are all right. Mary Kennedy lives in the same apartment building as you. I'm sure she would be happy to call you and drop by to see you if you needed her." Martha indicated that she thought this suggestion was a good one.

"Next," the counselor continued, "you still seem to be healthy and able to get about. Instead of staying in your room alone every day, why don't you busy yourself with other people who will make you feel needed. What about having one of the women who works at the church nursery pick you up two or three afternoons a week and let you help, perhaps by reading stories to the children after their naps?"

Martha was delighted with both suggestions. Within a month a number of little girls between the ages of three and six were calling her "Aunt Martha" and begging her to come and read stories every afternoon. Martha had no time to be lonely and it was obvious that she was needed in a special way by both the women at the nursery and the children. On the other hand, Mary Kennedy was pleased to be of help to Martha. Faithfully, she called her every day to see that she was all right.

3. *Feelings of uselessness* arise when many elderly men and women think that they are not needed. True, the elderly do not have the physical stamina to do many things that they could do in the past, but the carpenter, the bricklayer, the psychiatric nurse, the professional musician can find other ways to be useful after retiring. It is the counselor's job to show elderly people that they can still be

useful in life and can find new and different outlets for their talents and abilities as they grow older.

Several elderly people came to the pastor of a small rural church. Each in his or her own way expressed feelings of uselessness and not being needed. The pastor decided to get them together and help them form an Over-Sixty-Club. The men and women were pleased, for it gave them needed companionship with their peers and their own generation. They played cards together, prepared refreshments, and enjoyed each other's company. However, there still seemed to be something lacking. Horace and Helen came to the pastor to discuss the matter on behalf of the group: "We are glad," Helen began, "that you suggested forming our club; we enjoy each other's company and have fun, but something is missing and we don't know what it is."

It was clear to the counselor that they needed more than each other's company; they needed something to do to make them feel needed and useful. That is, he knew that groups, like individuals, need goals. He said to them: "I think you need some type of project so that you can use the talents and abilities that your group has. Why don't you consider doing something for the county orphanage and its children? You might go see Mrs. Wilson, the supervisor; she may have some suggestions."

A few months later, the Over-Sixty-Club meetings were filled with excited older men and women. On Mondays and Wednesdays the women had quilting bees; on Tuesdays and Thursdays they made clothes for the children. Before every holiday they made dolls for the children.

On Mondays and Wednesdays the men made new desks and bookshelves for the children's rooms. On Tuesdays and Thursdays the men taught craft skills to the children at the orphanage; for example, they taught them to lay new tile in their showers and a brick walk out front. Before holidays the men repaired toys for the children. They, along with the women, helped them decorate the orphanage.

Feeling needed is critically important to all people, especially to the elderly man and woman who often has to search harder for such opportunities.

4. *Fear of unwanted dependency* is one of the serious problems
for elderly men and women. There is an anxiety akin almost to ter-
ror at the thought of being helplessly thrown into a home or other
living situation where one is not wanted. This can be a son's home
in which the daughter-in-law simply despises, and loudly says so, the
elderly person living there. It is perhaps even more terrifying to be
"thrown" into an old folks' home where there is no relative to pro-
tect one against staff members who don't care and who may even
resent their duties toward the elderly and mistreat them as a result.

For example, a pastoral counselor was invited to the birthday
party for Cynthia, a seventy-one-year-old woman who lived alone.
She was a vivacious and active person with a vitality unique for persons her age. The pastoral counselor said to her: "Cynthia, I don't
know how you do it!" She replied: "I keep busy all the time and
find new interests every day. I don't feel lonely—but there is something I fear even worse—I fear unwanted dependency. I fear becoming an invalid and having to depend on my only son and his wife.
She and I never did hit it off very well. She's always complaining
how much my son and everyone else imposes on her. I pray God
will take me before I have to be dependent on her, for I know my
son would insist I come live with them if something happened to
me. Not that he would really want me either but he would think it
his duty to take care of me. No, sir, I don't want to be dependent
when I know I'm not wanted, but I wouldn't know how to avoid it
and this is what frightens me."

The pastoral counselor will often find, when dealing with such situations, that the best thing for him to do is to refer the elderly person to a different place to live—to a home where he or she is welcome. In order to do this, he must first gain an in-depth familiarity
with the resources for older people.

5. *Death* for the elderly must be faced in the near future and this
presents problems. Earlier in life people recognize that they must
die, but to younger men and women death is something to face in a
distant future. Not so with the aging; they must face the reality that
they will die in the not-too-distant future. The problem is they don't
know exactly when, and they find it difficult to maintain adequate
goal systems when they don't know how much time they have to

plan for or if they will have the physical strength to pursue their goals.

One elderly woman came to a counselor because of trouble with her daughter, with whom she was living: "I know it sounds kind of silly," she began, "but my daughter gets angry at me and we fight because I change my underwear twice every day. I guess it sounds crazy to you, but I know I've got to die one of these days and I wouldn't want to be caught in dirty underwear. Does this sound ridiculous to you?" The counselor assured her it did not. Later, he discussed the matter with the daughter, who admitted after the conversation she felt ashamed of herself for not understanding what the clean clothes meant to her mother.

A situation was described to a pastor by a man whose elderly wife had recently died. Three years before her death, the husband had bought his wife a pretty quilted bathrobe. Shortly before he bought it, the wife had been informed by her doctor that she had an incurable heart condition and that she would die within three or four years. On the night of her death, as she was having her fatal heart attack, she awakened her husband, who had been disappointed that she had never worn her robe, and asked him to bring it to her. She put it on, went into the living room, and sat down in her favorite chair. When her husband came into the room a few minutes later, she was dead in her rocking chair.

To repeat an important point, one's humanity in any growth or developmental phase is defined by his goals. This is no less important in the geriatric years than in any other. As noted above, there are special problems which are confronted by the elderly in setting up short-term and long-range goals.

For example, to the extent they are dependent on other people, they are not free to set many of their own goals or pursue many of the kinds of goals they would have earlier when they were more independent. To illustrate, today, in our highly mobile society the goals of many people involve the use of a car—going to games, to church, visiting friends, or working on various charity projects. The older person might still wish to do any or all of these, but he no longer has a car nor would his failing eyesight permit him to drive if he had one. If he is to pursue these goals, clearly someone else must solve the transportation problem. If this problem cannot be solved, the pastoral counselor must help them find other more realistic goals.

For example, Agnes talked to the pastoral counselor when he visited her in her daughter's home. "It's killing me that I can no longer take an active part in the DAR program in town, but we are six blocks from the bus stop and my daughter works and can't drive me. I used to be so active in all their projects and now I am sitting here with nothing to do."

The pastor contacted one of the directors of the local Books for the Blind program who went by and interviewed Agnes. Later the counselor learned that she was recording books for the blind and enjoying it thoroughly.

Long-range goals are as necessary to the elderly as they are to people at any other stage in life. They are especially important here because long-range goals can actually help keep them alive and will help obviate the tendency of the elderly to be negative when looking into their future. If they see no goals when they look into the future, they see only death.

For example, it is generally felt by historians that both Presidents John Adams and Thomas Jefferson were kept alive well after the time they would ordinarily have died because of their intense desire to live until the fiftieth anniversary of their signing of the Declaration of Independence. Both died on July 4, 1826; Jefferson died within minutes after asking a slave if it was yet midnight on July 3 and being told it was now July 4.

Often the pastoral counselor must help an elderly person overcome his natural reluctance to set long-range goals in the face of advancing age. It is important that he do so, however, because looking forward to the accomplishment of goals that may never be reached is healthier from a mental hygiene viewpoint than looking forward and seeing only death.

Undoubtedly, the pastor was of great help to Sydney, who was eighty years old, when he suggested that he tape record his memoirs for the use of his grandchildren and great-grandchildren during the long time he was just sitting and doing nothing. Sydney, as well as many other elderly people, took to this suggestion readily and to the surprise of everyone in his family. Although he never finished his memoirs, he stayed happy and alert and lived three years longer than the doctors said he would.

Conclusion

It is apparent that there is a great deal of counseling that a pastor may be asked to do both for elderly people and for those who must care for them. It has been shown that physical aging and rigid mental states and attitudes profoundly affect the personality of the elderly. It has been shown, further, that problems arise for the aging because of loss of security, feelings of uselessness, fear of isolation, fear of unwanted dependency, absence of goals, and because they must face death in the not-too-distant future. It is the pastor's duty not only to counsel the elderly man or woman to help them feel needed and wanted but also those who must care for them so that, above all, lines of communication can be improved which may help bridge the generation gaps between the elderly and those with whom they are associated.

9

THE DYING

Understanding the Dying

In some cases death is so sudden that there is no time for a pastoral counselor to be summoned. In other cases people die in a hospital or other institution where an institutional counselor is already available and is utilized. However, frequently death occurs in situations in which the pastor must function as the counselor, particularly in mission fields, isolated country areas, and often in cases with those who remain at home with a lingering terminal illness such as cancer. No group of individuals deserves the time of pastors more than the dying. No work is more delicate; none can be more gratifying. "Unfortunately," as an experienced nurse in a home for the elderly remarked, "even many clergymen seek to avoid the dying as much as they can. They project a fear of even talking to a dying person, possibly because such contact forces the counselor to face, realistically, that he, too, must die sometime."

The intensity of the fear of dying varies with different people. Sometimes it is missing altogether. Generally speaking, any fear is inversely proportionate to the dying person's belief that he or she has achieved in life something of importance to himself or has had rewarding interpersonal relationships and/or a belief in a satisfying life after death.

It is not uncommon for a counselor to hear something similar to this: "I'm not afraid to die. Jim and I had a beautiful life together. We raised three fine children who are happily married, with lovely families of their own, and, you know, I somehow look forward to joining Jim in heaven."

It can be painful for the counselor to help some other dying individuals as the two illustrations that follow indicate.

A pastor talked with a young woman who was an orphan and had never married. She was in a hospital dying of leukemia. "Please," she begged, "don't let me die. I don't want to die. No one has ever loved me. I've been alone all my life and now I'm going to die and be in the grave alone. I just can't stand it." Her youth had nothing to do with this woman's desolation. Dying and losing her last chance to have any warm and meaningful interpersonal relationship caused her extreme distress and pain as she lay dying.

It was equally painful to counsel and console a young boy of fourteen in the same hospital who had damaged, critically, what turned out to be his only kidney in a football scrimmage. He screamed, before dying: "I don't want to die; I'm too young . . . Please, don't let me die. I haven't lived yet."

The pastor hurt within himself, but he did not turn away from these two or cease to counsel them. One of his principal tasks was to assist them as they were dying to alleviate their despair. He did not know, anymore than the two who were dying, why they should have to die so young; however, he chose to talk about other things.

He let them know that he shared their agony and pain and that he felt helpless to do anything but love them. Most important, he shared an intimate and significant experience with both of them. It was not by verbal counseling. As each died he simply held their hands. He knew he had conveyed to them that they were dying loved and that they were important and would be missed. Knowing this, the counselor felt that they were consoled and their pain eased.

Needs of the Dying

The needs of the dying are many and varied. Most of the dying with whom the pastoral counselor will be called upon to serve will be the elderly, unlike the two illustrations above. He must (1) as above, show love for the dying by not being afraid to be with and talk to the dying person and must understand the need for someone to be honest; he must (2) assist the elderly dying person to plan his funeral when there is time and to put his affairs in order; and he must (3) finally assist the person to avoid despair by helping him look toward a rewarding life after death or to contemplate the accomplishments and love he or she has known in the past, or both.

To illustrate, a doctor came to his pastor, a Roman Catholic priest. He began: "I don't know whether you know Mrs. Armstead—she lives on the other side of the lake. She was born a Roman Catholic but she hasn't been to church for years. Her husband is Catholic but he doesn't practice the faith either. They have two boys in their late teens. I suspect the last time Louise and her husband were in church was at the baptism of her youngest son. Anyway, I haven't told her but she has a breast cancer which has metastasized. She may live three months, but I doubt if she'll live any longer. You might want to go see her."

The priest knew that it was his duty to visit the woman and counsel her if possible. His reception by Louise was somewhat cool. As she told him: "Ted and I broke with the church when Ted's sister divorced her husband and wanted Father Smith, who was here before you, to perform the marriage ceremony for her and her present husband. He refused and they had to get married before a J.P. My husband was furious and we quit going to Mass and receiving the Sacraments." She paused and then added, almost wistfully and with a sigh: "I kinda miss my church even after these many years. I used to be president of the young ladies' sodality."

After several visits, the counselor found that communication between Louise and himself had become increasingly warm. One month later he came to her home and found her bedridden. It was obvious she was in a great deal of pain but she remarked: "It's so good to have someone to talk to. My husband and sons are gone all day and somehow even my old friends don't visit me very often." She added, significantly, "Some of them seem almost afraid to come to see me."

She paused for a while and then added: "Father, am I going to die . . . aren't a lot of my friends staying away because they think

I'm dying and are afraid to be here?" The priest had consulted the doctor; both felt it would do no harm—in fact, it might do some good —for the priest to be honest with the woman and tell her she was dying, so he answered: "Yes, Louise, you have a terminal cancer, the doctor tells me." Surprisingly, instead of being upset, Louise sighed and then answered very calmly: "I've known it for a long time; why couldn't they be honest with me? I appreciate your telling me, Father . . . Do you have any idea about how long I've got left?" He told her the doctor thought about a month.

Louise seemed revitalized. She immediately said: "O.K., Father, we have a lot to do in this short time—will you help me? And when you come again will you bring the Blessed Sacrament and hear my confession?" He agreed to do anything that he could. One important thing was to help her look back and see what she had accomplished and the love she had shared not only with her husband and sons but with many friends.

In the weeks that followed she and the counselor made plans for her funeral and she instructed her husband concerning the disposition of other personal things. From time to time she wondered aloud what her last moments would be like. The counselor asked the doctor to explain this to her, which he did.

The day before she died, although in severe pain and looking emaciated, she greeted the priest with a faint but beautiful smile. She asked, "Father, will you bring Communion not only for me but for my husband and two sons when you come tomorrow?" The next day Louise, her husband, and two sons went to Confession and received Holy Communion. Shortly thereafter she died peacefully, with her husband and sons kneeling at her bedside, answering the prayers as the priest administered Extreme Unction and said the prayers for the dying.

Counseling the family of the dying, especially young children in the family, challenges the skill of pastoral counselors. It challenges the skill of the pastor because he must deal, here, with an age group whose theology is immature and undeveloped by definition. As with counseling with anyone, the pastor must work within the framework of the client's theology, not his own.

Caroline Becket, a nineteen-year-old member of the congregation, came to her pastor for assistance. "Brother Jones, you've got to help me. I'm afraid my new family are becoming bitter and in danger of losing their faith in God." Caroline was a devout Methodist and faithful member of her Church. She had been married at sixteen; when she was nineteen, her husband died leaving her with a nine-month-old baby. On the day she buried her husband, her widowed mother died, leaving five younger brothers and sisters for her to raise. The day she buried her mother she asked the pastor to come and talk with the children.

"I'll miss my husband and my mother, but I really believe that all things work together for good to them that love the Lord, and I couldn't love the Lord more. My brothers and sisters that I'm raising don't have that kind of faith, though, and they often come in from school crying because God is letting everyone else have a father but took theirs. Last night at supper the youngest said, 'I don't love God anymore. He's a mean man.' To my surprise the older children agreed. The oldest girl said, 'If He's such a good God, He sure has a funny way of showing it.' I'm just panicked, Brother Jones. I couldn't have survived the last few months without my strong faith in God. I know how important it will be to them to hold on to theirs, but I'm afraid I'm not doing much good with this right now. I'm going to have to ask your help."

The pastor told her that a sustained faith in God depended on trust in God's ultimate goodness and love. "Tell them," he said, "that there are many things that they will not completely understand in life as they did not understand death. But they can be sure that God, who loved them enough to create them as His special children, would do nothing that was not ultimately for their good and that they must always trust Him to do so."

A popular saying is "there are no atheists in fox holes"—that is that when one is faced with possible death, he turns back to his religion. Contrary to this assumption, many people arrive at the time of death who profess no faith but have made their peace with death. When the counselor visits this kind of person, he is not needed as a counselor, as such, but he can still make an important contribution as a person by being a warm, concerned, understanding friend.

Conclusion

In summary, the pastoral counselor can be of service in many ways
to the dying and their loved ones. He can assist both young and old
to alleviate despair, prepare for death as far as possible, and meet
any spiritual needs they have. In all cases, he must convey to the
dying as well as the living personal warmth, friendship, and understanding.

In all cases, he must assist the loved ones to adjust to a life without the deceased.

III

Pastoral Counseling and Spiritual and Moral Values

10

SPIRITUAL AND MORAL VALUES

Introduction

Throughout this book it has been indicated that the special role of the pastoral counselor is to assist clients in matters related to spiritual and moral values. Specifically, the counselor's role is to help them to define and comprehend their values rationally; in terms of goals and consequences to their lives, to help them evaluate these values; and to teach them the necessity of constant reassessment of these values as they grow and mature as human beings. Certain logical questions arise as a result: How does the counselor fulfill this role and what techniques does he use to assist a client in recognizing, evaluating and determining his on-going value system? This chapter will address itself to these practical questions.

Principles, Guidelines, and Assumptions

Before techniques to be used by the pastoral counselor in particular cases can be illustrated, it is necessary for the counselor to understand certain principles, guidelines, and assumptions.

1. All human beings live by value systems whether they are aware of it or not. Even though the value systems and the philosophies and

theologies behind them may not be explicit or clearly defined in the mind of an individual, they are operative. Everything experienced in a person's life influences his spiritual and moral value system. Included are individual and group needs, interests, desires, aspirations, goals, objectives, and prejudices, to name but a few. These and other factors influence what a person believes—his spiritual value system— and based on what he believes, his moral value system automatically follows. In the normal course of things, one's moral and spiritual values are, typically, acquired in a very haphazard way and with little conscious thought. As such, they contain many inconsistencies, contradictions, inadequacies, and gaps that create tension in the individual when his life experiences are not consistent with his amorphous theology. The pastoral counselor must understand that the mental health of a client is not predictably stable in the presence of such a theological nonsystem. As a result, he must help the client to derive a theology for himself which is consistent within itself, reflects reality as the client experiences it, and has no gaps by which his experience cannot be explained.

In summary, the client, with the help of the counselor, must substitute an inadequate, unthought-out theology with a rational systematic theology.

2. The pastoral counselor, unlike other counselors, is uniquely concerned with spiritual values and moral values. If he does not take care of these, no one else is going to do so because no other type of counselor is trained to do this. As indicated in (1) above, he will assist the client to develop a systematic theology for the client's use. In doing this, he is concerned, among other things, about a person's ontological and teleological beliefs as they relate to himself, to others, and all creation. A pastor must understand the client's beliefs about the source of his and all life, its nature, and the purpose for existence and the client's concepts regarding the final end of all creation. The pastor must therefore take into account the client's belief or nonbelief in a God, his concept of who or what God is if he believes God exists, his belief or lack of belief in life after death, and his belief regarding any reward or punishment system that may exist here or in the hereafter. The counselor must determine the client's convictions regarding the human person, that is, is he simply an ani-

mal, a composite of body and soul, potentially an immortal being, a reincarnated bullfrog, or something else. He must ascertain what the client feels is the purpose of existence and what part he feels he, other people, and all creation play in a possible Divine Plan—if he believes such a plan exists. In short, the counselor is guided in his counseling by the client's spiritual beliefs regarding the source, nature, and purpose of himself, of others, and of any supernatural beings he believes exist.

To restate, the counselor helps the client to answer the simple, yet profound, questions: "Who am I? Where did I come from? Why am I here? And where am I going?" Having to some degree answered these questions, the client has developed at least the nucleus of his systematic theology. The nature of his concept of the Supreme Being, either as a supernatural being or beings or as man himself, and its influence on his present and future life, determine his spiritual value system and, subsequently, his moral value system.

As was said above, each man's moral value system is dependent on and stems from his spiritual value system. These moral values, in turn, determine the conduct and behavior an individual feels he should follow. Hence, what one believes—his spiritual value system— determines what he feels he should do—his moral value system; and on the basis of these moral values, he selects his behavior and judges his conduct—and often the conduct of others—as being morally right or wrong or morally indifferent.

Since spiritual value systems are different for every individual, moral value systems also differ. They are as divergent as the system that leads the hedonist, who is his own "Supreme Being," to self-indulgent behavior based on his philosophy that one should "eat, drink, and be merry for tomorrow you may die," and the altruistic and self-sacrificing, self-giving of a Christian missionary in Africa, who believes in the Christian God as the Supreme Being. The missionary does not look for any reward in this life but the satisfaction that he or she has done those things that will enable her to enjoy an everlasting, blissful life in heaven. Both are behaving morally within their spiritual value systems. The counselor must deal with both cases and with degrees of difference in between as well, as totally different value systems. He must accept any and all such systems.

3. Just as the pastor in his role as counselor does not concern himself about the morality of a client's behavior as such but is concerned about the client as a person, he does not evaluate the content of a client's spiritual and moral value systems on the basis of his own system of morality. He must assist the client to understand, evaluate, affirm, reject, or refine his own personal spiritual value system and his moral value systems. Although the counselor will have his own value systems, he will have to act as an educator and teacher by sharing ideas from numerous theological systems, not just his own. A pastor, therefore, should be able to counsel professionally and effectively a Protestant, a Roman Catholic, a Hindu, an agnostic, an atheist, a monist, a deist, a humanist, or a pantheist when problems are brought to him involving the person's specific moral and spiritual value systems. If he cannot be objective because of his own prejudices or values, he should disqualify himself and refer the client to another counselor. If he cannot give information because of lack of knowledge on his own part, he should either learn the facts or, again, refer the client. In addition, the counselor in working with other theological systems other than his own will very quickly find any gaps, inconsistencies, and inadequacies that may be present in his own system and these will cause him anxiety and conflict. It follows that a pastoral counselor must have a well-defined system theology of his own.

4. Basic to the above counseling in the areas of spiritual and moral values must be the assumption that everyone evaluates, modifies, and redevelops his spiritual and moral value systems in terms of his own need for self-fulfillment and self-actualization. That is, in terms of his own particular personal needs, prejudices, interests, background, outlook, goals, and desires to achieve self-esteem and the esteem of others, to form the interpersonal relationships he wants, and find self-actualization either in this life or in a life after death.

To illustrate, St. Francis, who sold all that he had and spent his life at great personal sacrifice ministering to the poor, insisted that behind even the most seemingly altruistic and selfless behavior of any person there was a "Holy Selfishness" based on the primal need of any human to fulfill himself according to his own personal concepts of self-actualization, regardless of anything or anyone else or of any creed, code, or cult.

Christ Himself affirmed that in the Christian spiritual and moral value systems, self-love—properly understood—must come before love of neighbor. By implication, He declared that man is not able to love God or his neighbor unless he loves himself. Such love is not possible unless founded upon moral and spiritual value systems which place the individual's self-fulfillment and self-actualization above all other considerations.

Hence, to assist a client in matters related to his spiritual and moral value systems, a pastor must seek to learn as much as he can about the on-going personal needs, aspirations, interests, desires, and motivations of the individual. He must understand, further, that there are no two people alike in terms of what will fulfill them as persons, and therefore, no two spiritual and moral value systems can be exactly alike. This means that the counselor must be flexible enough to work within various value systems and recognize that the old practice of imposing value systems is maladaptive within the counseling process.

5. As was said above, an individual's behavior stems from his value system. It is important in the counseling process to note that conflicting aspirations can frequently stem from the same values. This conflict may well be brought to the pastoral counselor. For example, it is not uncommon for a young Roman Catholic boy to ask for assistance in answering the question: "In which way can I serve God best—by becoming a celibate priest or by marrying and raising a Christian family?" Or again, the young man studying for the Protestant ministry may ask for counseling in deciding the right answer to this question: "Shall I go to the mission field and gain merit and God's blessing for living a life of heroic isolation in a jungle, or will it be equally rewarding to me personally, and please God as much, if I take a church and work to save the souls of members of a rich congregation on New York's Fifth Avenue?" The values are the same, but the behaviors are in stark competition. The pastor's role is to assist such individuals to determine the behavior which will be relatively more self-fulfilling while at the same time serving God. This

action can be facilitated by following another guideline for pastoral counseling. It is one of the most important.

6. In assisting a client to choose between goals in his on-going evaluation of his whole spiritual and moral value systems, it is essential that the pastor help the client assess the over-all cost to himself of accepting one goal rather than another, that is, to help him assess the reward and punishment as the client perceives them.

In addition to considering the relative merits of competing goals based on the same values, people also reassess the values along the same line. The pastor can play an important role here also. He must help anyone evaluating his or her value systems to answer these fundamental questions: "What has it cost me to maintain my spiritual and moral value systems? What have been the rewards? Was it worth it or should I change?"

For example, Paul, an intern in a hospital for incurable diseases, came to his pastor for counseling about a conflict in his moral values. Paul said: "Three times this week I have been working with every means at my command to prolong the life of patients while they beg me to please let them die. I believe life is sacred and everyone has a reason for being here and a job to do for God, and since I cannot know when that job is finished—even if it is just witnessing to the person in the next bed—I can't bring myself to let them die if I can possibly avoid it. On the other hand, I can't stand seeing people in such agony and pain for what may be no good reason."

The pastor discovered, as is frequently the case, that the intern had an even more deep-seated conflict, which involved his spiritual values and even his theology itself. Paul's concept of an omnipotent, all-loving God was in conflict with the helpless pain he daily saw among his patients. The counselor knew that if he helped Paul resolve his theological conflict, the resolution of his conflicts in values would resolve themselves.

Paul decided, after several sessions, that his omnipotent God had chosen to limit his power once He had set his creation in motion, but never ceased to love and be concerned about the children He had created. Using this theology as a basis, he decided each patient had a right to exercise the power God had relinquished to them and to choose to die when they wished to do so.

Principles for Counseling

The three major principles upon which a client's spiritual and moral value systems should be founded are that the systems (1) must foster creativity, (2) must be energizing, and (3) must be sustaining. They must avoid the converses: namely, they (1) must not foster boredom or unproductiveness, (2) must avoid emotions such as anxiety, fear, and depression that deplete energy, and (3) must not be destructive.

In addition the counselor should keep in mind that any client's systems must be evaluated in terms of their effect not only on him and his life but on his world.

The following illustrations suggest some ways for the client, with the help of the counselor, to evaluate his value systems and subsequent behavior.

1. Alvin, a teenage boy, remained after Sunday school to talk to his teacher who was also a counselor in the high school he attended. "I'm so miserable I had to talk to someone. Will you please not tell my mother and dad? I wouldn't only get a lickin' but probably would have to go to bed for a week without supper as punishment. I guess I'm going to hell. I feel terrible. You see, I know I'm no good. I'm a hypocrite. I pretend to believe all the religious teaching my mother and father hold and those of our minister who I really don't like. Well, Miss Jenkins, I've had it up to here, I can't take it anymore. I'm sick of hearing about a God who is a stern old man with a white beard sitting on a throne ready to strike you dead if you don't mind him. I've heard about the wrath of God until I can't stand it. Who wants to go to a heaven and spend eternity playing harps and bowing and scraping to such a God? All I hear is punishment, sin, punishment, sin . . . I know it's probably wrong to say it, but I think my dad feels he has to play God for us children. He rarely has a kind thing to say, but he's quick to bring out his leather belt and use it on us when, as he says 'Alvin, you have transgressed the laws of God and man. It is my duty to punish you here so that you can avoid eternal punishment hereafter.' I even got beaten the other day because someone, not me, left the faucet on the outside of

the house running, and when I told my dad I didn't do it, he said, 'Now I must punish you not only for what you did, but for telling a lie.' I really got a belting. I guess I will just run away and wait to go to hell."

By any of the three principles mentioned above, the counselor knew that the theology Alvin was running from was inadequate for him in terms of his humanity. Not only did it discourage creativity, but it also was energy-depleting and destructive. He was cowering in fear.

The counselor allowed Alvin to continue talking and pouring out his negative feelings. When he had apparently exhausted them, she counseled him: "First of all, Alvin, I am pleased and honored that you came to me with your problem. I shall do all that I can to help you. Let me say one thing before we get to the main problem: it is quite normal and natural for a teenage boy or girl to question the religious tenets and beliefs he or she thinks parents and other adults hold. I think it is good and constructive, for it can mean that the boy or girl is growing up and trying to develop his or her own spiritual and moral value system. So don't be disturbed that you are questioning what you see as the moral and spiritual values of your parents and of our conservative minister."

She paused, then continued: "Alvin, you've told me all the things you don't like about religion. Can you think of anything you do like?"

Alvin thought for a while. As a slight smile came on his face, he said: "Yes, there are some things I like. One thing sticks out in my mind especially. About six months ago an old minister who had been a missionary in Uganda preached the seven o'clock evening service. Never once did I hear him say anything about the wrath of God. Instead, he talked about Jesus. How he was God but became a man and how he loved everybody. He made me feel—it's hard to explain —all warm inside and not quite so lonely. That's the kind of God I could believe in and love."

Miss Jenkins said nothing for a few minutes while the tears welled up in Alvin's eyes. She knew that he was emotionally describing a loving, sustaining God. When he had spent this emotion, she continued: "Alvin, I was reading one of our church magazines the other day and it told about one of the great Christians named

Augustine. He made a point that impressed me. He preached that there are many reasons for being religious but there are two main ones—fear of punishment, which is basically, in my opinion, destructive to one's humanity, or love, which energizes and sustains. From what you've said, although I'm no judge, it seems your parents consider fear of punishment a principal reason for being religious. From what you say, the emphasis in your spiritual and moral value systems should be love."

In the weeks that followed, Alvin and Miss Jenkins had many conversations. She helped Alvin find his own moral and spiritual value systems based upon his principal concern that love should be its foundation. She was able to show him that he could respect his parents' moral and spiritual value systems since they seemed to work for them, although, both knew they would not satisfy or work for Alvin.

Miss Jenkins lost track of Alvin for a number of years. She heard that he not only became a doctor but an ordained minister. In her old age she was happy to receive a letter from Alvin who was, at the time, serving as a medical missionary in a remote area in the Philippines. His letter said: "I've decided the situation here is hell enough without looking any further for one. And I am here, by God's Good Grace, to do everything I can about it so that the people here can experience God's love for them and not just be told about it." He thanked her for helping him avoid what would be for him a destructive theology and for helping him develop one which would sustain him and encourage him to live a constructive, creative, energizing life.

2. The warden at a state penitentiary called the prison chaplain one day to ask a favor. "Henry, I wish you'd do me a favor and go see this new prisoner who was admitted last week. His name is Alfonso Peres. He's twenty years old and has been, I understand, labeled a sociopath. That means that he cannot or does not feel for other people and he does not learn from experience. He comes from a tough neighborhood in the Bronx. He's lived on the street all his life. Neither he nor anyone else knows where his parents are. He's been in trouble since he was ten years old—fights, stealing, all sorts of trouble. Finally, a family took him in, to act as his foster parents.

The woman had a lot of expensive jewelry. One evening when the foster parents were out, he, with the help of two men, took the jewelry and sold it to a fence for one tenth of what it was worth. Alfonso pretended that he was forced at gunpoint to let the two men into the house and that he had nothing to do with the theft. One of the two, however, implicated Alfonso. The judge gave him two years for grand larceny. Well, the reason I'm calling is that no one seems to be able to get to this man. I'm afraid he's going to get hurt if he doesn't shape up. Also, I think they've got him pegged wrong. I don't think he's a sociopath; he just hasn't had a chance."

The chaplain agreed to see Alfonso. Everyday, he made it a point to go by and say hello to the man. For two months he got nothing but a grunt back. The chaplain did not push; it would have done no good.

One night the chaplain heard that Alfonso had been badly beaten by other inmates of the prison. He went to the hospital ward of the prison. It was obvious from the cuts on his face and bruises on his body that Alfonso was in great pain. Each day Henry visited him, but there was still no conversation.

Two weeks went by. Alfonso was then able to sit in a chair. To the surprise of the chaplain, Alfonso broke the silence one day and said: "Hey, could I rap with you sometime?" "How about now?" Henry asked. "It's okay with me," Alfonso replied. Then he continued.

"Well, I ain't good at talk but I gotta do something; I'm fed up. No matter what I do, I end up on the short end of the stick. It just ain't worth it. I'm tired of livin' in jails and eatin' out of garbage cans. Do you dig what I'm sayin', man?" The chaplain assured him he did.

The chaplain recognized that Alfonso's value system, such as it was, was one that Alfonso was ready to reject because of the punishments it involved without compensating rewards. It was Henry's task to help the man develop a rewarding moral value system.

After a few months the chaplain felt free enough to say to Alfonso: "So you don't like the way your life's been going and you're tired of jails and prisons. You know, the way you have been living only leads to trouble. You've got to change your whole way of looking at things and acting."

Alfonso sat quietly for a while, then said: "How do I do it?" This gave the chaplain a chance to suggest that he get his high school equivalency while in prison and, with a new moral value system they would work out together, begin to plan a more rewarding future.

The chaplain had found in these discussions that Alfonso had no religious beliefs, having rejected the destructive system he had learned in his foster home. He indicated to the counselor that the system had been mostly negative and it was more valuable for him not to believe because then he would not incur the responsibility inherent in that system. He had arrived at the prison with no theological system, and therefore it was not surprising that his behavior was destructive, erratic, and apparently amoral.

In their discussions, the chaplain discussed numerous theological systems and pointed out how each could bring order to Alfonso's nonfocused life.

For the first time in his life, Alfonso began to discuss realistically what he wanted out of life and to develop a value system that was not only consistent with his life's goals but also would aid him in achieving them.

Five years after he left the prison, Alfonso was constructively serving as a rehabilitation counselor for delinquent boys in a reform school and had found that his own happiness was predicated, often, on the happiness of others.

3. A middlescent woman lay sick with hepatitis in a ward of a city hospital. The nurse, a Roman Catholic nun, who was also a skilled counselor, attended her.

One day the woman said: "I'd like to talk to you about something that's serious to me. I'm forty-eight years old and I've led a helluva life. My mother, like me, was a prostitute and my father a drunk. I've got a lot of brothers and sisters, but I don't know where they are. I've got no religion, and I don't believe there's a God or a hereafter. All I've got to look forward to is a few more years, and I want them to be happy. They sure haven't been in the past. You see, I was a pretty good-looking gal when I was young. I decided I could make a lot of money selling myself. I did pretty well when I was in my twenties and early thirties. It got more and more difficult as I got older. Finally, I had to get a pimp and work night and day. I've been beat up, knocked around, and kicked by my customers. I've had VD at least ten times. Now I've got this damned hepatitis. I'm sick of the whole mess. Do you think it's too late for me to change?"

The counselor could easily see that this woman was not living an emotionally creative, sustaining existence, but to the contrary was emotionally drained and had no constructive goals to look forward to. There were no satisfying rewards in her life.

The nurse assured her it was never too late. She indicated to her that she needed to reject her old value system and adopt a new one which could bring her rewards rather than the punishments she had experienced. Together they helped formulate a new code of behavior for her, based on new moral and spiritual values with new goals and objectives. After hospitalization, she went to work in the day and attended night nursing training. Later she became a nursing assistant in a hospital. She cared for the girls and women who suffered from the same diseases she had known. She spent the rest of her life in caring for these sick women. For her the work was both creative and emotionally sustaining.

4. A middlescent man named Albert, with a problem of alcoholism, lay in his cot after having experienced DTs for the first time. He felt miserable, jumpy, and sick. He had been in the treatment center before—in fact, many times—but this was the first time he had experienced the agony he now felt. He liked to drink, but he didn't like it to affect him this way.

The following day his pastor visited him. Albert began to explain to him what had happened: "You see, I must have been ill. Ordinarily I can drink and it doesn't hit me this way. I probably need to see my doctor and have a check-up. I'm probably run down."

The pastor said: "Albert, I've known you a long time. I think we've been good friends. I'm not going to ask you how many days you have missed work in the past year because the booze happened to hit you. I'm not a professional in the field, so I don't know and have no idea if you have a chronic problem of alcoholism or not. What I do know, however, is that your drinking has been destructive, not only in putting you here in the hospital but in terms of getting you fired from a job you've had ten years and losing many of your friends for you. In addition, I have a painful job to do. I hope you will understand. Your wife, Edna, asked me to tell you that she really means it this time; it's got to be the bottle or her. Think about it and I'll be back tomorrow."

The pastor returned the next day. Albert began: "Parson, I like to drink; I'd sure hate to give it up, but I sure don't want to lose Edna either. I don't want to make a choice between them. Do you suppose you could convince Edna that from now on, if she will stick with me, I'll control my drinking so it won't interfere with our lives? Would you try to convince her, parson? It would be doing me a big favor."

The pastor said: "Albert, I have no doubt that you get pleasure, at least at times, from your drinking, but now it's a question of values. Which do you want, the bottle or Edna? I'm convinced you can't have both. I can't make a decision for you but I think it is a question of relative values. Which do you value more?"

"But," Albert protested, "I want both. I want to feel free to drink in my own home and have Edna there."

Albert left the treatment center without making a decision. Only after he was almost killed while driving his car did he finally say to the counselor: "You're right, and I thank God I have had one more chance to decide what is right and wrong for me. With Edna's help, I've decided what is important and what is less important. I'll try my darnedest to be a good husband in the future, for that means a lot to me. I'm glad you didn't let me duck the decision I had to make. Thanks a lot."

The counselor, with the permission of Albert, met with both him and Edna. The three of them sought and found ways in which the husband and wife could live a creative, sustaining, and energizing family life. Albert found this life more than supplanted the need to drink excessively.

5. Jack Saxby came to his pastor. His wife had been killed the week before in an automobile accident when a hot-rodding teenager on pot ran into her car. His hurt had turned to anger. He shouted at the pastor: "I've always had faith in God, but what kind of God is it that would take Cynthia in the prime of her life and leave me and

the three kids without a wife and mother. I really wonder if there's a God at all!"

The pastor could see that Jack's concept of God was not sustaining him in this hour of crisis. Further, his questioning of God at the time was not a constructive but destructive one.

"Obviously, Jack, your faith is not sustaining you in this hour of need. Further, I don't think it is going to be helpful for you to reconstruct your beliefs while you are caught up in such emotional pain and loss." The pastor had learned, from experience, to discourage clients from reassessing their value systems in times of emotional crisis. He always made it a point to help a person reassess his values when time had had a chance to heal the pain, but not before.

In later discussions the pastor pointed out to Jack that a system of belief which could not sustain one in the hour of crisis was not adequate. He then assisted Jack to develop a concept of God that could fulfill this need.

7. An elderly judge seventy-five years of age came to a pastoral counselor and said: "I have certain misgivings about my proposed marriage to an eighteen-year-old lady I've been seeing. I have never been so happy in my life. I'm so full of energy, I feel like a sixteen-year-old kid at times, and I'm doing more cases in a week now than I used to do in a month."

The pastor asked: "And what are your misgivings?"

"I worry about her youth. I wonder if she should spend her time with an old man like me rather than with people her own age and what kind of security she can feel married to a man who cannot have much longer to live. I also worry about what her friends will say, to say nothing of what I know the parents feel now. I've also wondered if I can make such a young girl happy as a husband?"

It was clear to the counselor that this relationship for the judge was creative, energizing, and sustaining, but it was not clear at all in the larger view of the judge's world—which included the girl, her friends, and her family—that it might not be destructive over-all. His counseling involved, as in every case, getting the client to look at the total picture and not the picture just in terms of his own wants and needs.

Conclusion

It has been indicated that a client's behavior is based upon his moral and spiritual value systems which in turn are predicated on his religious beliefs, either thought out or implied.

The pastoral counselor must help a client not only to define his systems but also to re-evaluate his systems from time to time in view of his on-going life experiences.

This re-evaluation of the elements in the systems, in turn, should be based upon an objective evaluation of whether these elements are supportive of creativity and whether they energize and sustain not only the client but essential elements, including people, in his world.

On the other hand, even though the behavior arising from a client's beliefs may be creative and sustaining to the larger world around him, if it is destructive to him personally, it is clearly predicated on inadequate value systems for him, and the pastor must assist him to find systems which are adequate both for himself and his world.

BIBLIOGRAPHY

I

PASTORAL COUNSELING

Aldrich, Clarence Knight. *A Pastoral Counseling Casebook.* Philadelphia: Westminster Press, 1968.

Bordin, Edward S. *Psychological Counseling.* New York: Appleton-Century-Crofts, 1968.

Brammer, Lawrence M. *The Helping Relationship: Process and Skills.* Englewood Cliffs, N.J.: Prentice-Hall, 1973.

———, and Everett L. Shostrom. *Therapeutic Psychology: Fundamentals of Actualization Counseling and Psychotherapy,* 2d ed. Englewood Cliffs, N.J.: Prentice-Hall, 1968.

Carkhuff, Robert R. *Helping and Human Relations: A Primer for Lay and Professional Helpers.* New York: Holt, Rinehart and Winston, 1969.

Cavanaugh, John R. *Fundamental Pastoral Counseling.* Milwaukee: Bruce Publishing Company, 1962.

Clinebell, Howard John. *Basic Types of Pastoral Counseling.* Nashville: Abingdon Press, 1966.

Coleman, James C. *Abnormal Psychology in Modern Life,* 3d ed. Chicago: Scott, Foresman, 1964.

Combs, Arthur W., Donald L. Avila, and William W. Pukey. *Helping Relationships: Basic Concepts for the Helping Professions.* Boston: Allyn and Bacon, 1971.

Cottle, William C., and N. M. Downie. *Procedures and Preparation for Counseling.* Englewood Cliffs, N.J.: Prentice-Hall, 1960.

Curran, Charles Arthur. *Counseling and Psychotherapy: The Pursuit of Values.* New York: Sheed and Ward, 1968.
———. *Personality Factors in Counseling.* New York: Grune and Stratton, 1945.
———. *Religious Values in Counseling and Psychotherapy.* New York: Sheed and Ward, 1969.
Delaney, Daniel J., and Sheldon Eisenberg. *The Counseling Process.* Chicago: Rand McNally, 1972.
Dicks, Russell Leslie. *Principles and Practices of Pastoral Care.* Englewood Cliffs, N.J.: Prentice-Hall, 1963.
Elbert, Edmund J. *I Understand: A Handbook for Counseling in the Seventies.* New York: Sheed and Ward, 1971.
Godin, André. *The Pastor as Counselor,* trans. by Bernard Phillips. New York: Holt, Rinehart and Winston, 1965.
Hagmaier, George, and Robert W. Gleason. *Counseling the Catholic.* New York: Sheed and Ward, 1959.
Hauck, Paul A. *Reason in Pastoral Counseling.* Philadelphia: Westminster Press, 1972.
Hiltner, Seward. *The Counselor in Counseling: Case Notes in Pastoral Counseling.* New York: Abingdon-Cokesbury Press, 1952.
Hostie, Raymond. *Pastoral Counseling,* trans. by Gilbert Barth, New York: Sheed and Ward, 1966.
Howe, Reul H. *The Miracle of Dialogue.* Greenwich, Conn.: Seabury Press, 1963.
Hulme, William Edward. *Pastoral Care Come of Age.* Nashville: Abingdon Press, 1970.
Kell, Bill L., and William J. Mueller. *Impact and Change: A Study of Counseling Relationships.* New York: Appleton-Century-Crofts, 1966.
Kemp, Charles F. *A Pastoral Counseling Guidebook.* Nashville: Abingdon Press, 1971.
Klink, Thomas W. *Depth Perspectives in Pastoral Work.* Englewood Cliffs, N.J.: Prentice-Hall, 1965.
Laplace, Jean. *The Direction of Conscience,* trans. by John C. Guinness. New York: Herder and Herder, 1965.
Leach, Max. *Christianity and Mental Health.* Dubuque, Iowa: William C. Brown, 1969.
McIntosh, Ian F. *Pastoral Care and Pastoral Theology.* Philadelphia: Westminster Press, 1972.
McLemore, Clinton W. *Clergyman's Psychological Handbook.* Grand Rapids, Mich.: Eerdmans, 1974.
Maher, Trafford P. *Self, A Measureless Sea: Counseling Theory and Practice.* St. Louis: Catholic Hospital Association, 1966.
Maslow, A. H. *Motivation and Personality.* New York: Harper, 1954.

May, Rollo. *The Art of Counseling: How to Gain and Give Mental Health.* Nashville: Cokesbury Press, 1939.

Mowrer, Orval Hobart. *The Crisis in Psychiatry and Religion.* Princeton, N.J.: Van Nostrand, 1961.

Oates, Wayne Edward. *New Dimensions in Pastoral Care.* Philadelphia: Fortress Press, 1970.

———. *Pastoral Counseling.* Philadelphia: Westminster Press, 1974.

O'Brien, Michael J. *An Introduction to Pastoral Counseling.* Staten Island, N.Y.: Alba House, 1968.

Patterson, C. H. *Theories of Counseling and Psychotherapy,* 2d ed. New York: Harper & Row, 1973.

Pietrofesa, John J., George E. Leonard, and William Van Hoose. *The Authentic Counselor.* Chicago: Rand McNally, 1971.

Pond, Desmond. *Counseling in Religion and Psychiatry.* London: Oxford University Press, 1973.

Simons, Joseph B., and Jeanne Reidy. *The Human Art of Counseling.* New York: Herder and Herder, 1971.

Snoeck, André. *Confession and Pastoral Psychology,* trans. by Theodore Zuydwijk. Westminster, Md.: Newman Press, 1961.

Switzer, David K. *The Minister as Crisis Counselor.* Nashville: Abingdon Press, 1974.

Tyler, Leona E. *The Work of the Counselor.* New York: Appleton-Century-Crofts, 1969.

Van Kaam, Adrian L. *The Art of Existential Counseling.* Wilkes-Barre, Pa.: Dimension Books, 1966.

Vander Veldt, James H. *Pyschology for Counselors.* Chicago: Franciscan Herald Press, 1971.

Whitlock, Glenn E. *Preventive Psychology and the Church.* Philadelphia: Westminster Press, 1973.

II

PASTORAL COUNSELING AND
HUMAN MATURATION AND DEVELOPMENT

Autton, Norman. *The Pastoral Care of the Dying.* London: S.P.C.K., 1966.

Bachmann, C. Charles. *Ministering to the Grief Sufferer.* Englewood Cliffs, N.J.: Prentice-Hall, 1964.

Bassett, William T. *Counseling the Childless Couple.* Englewood Cliffs, N.J.: Prentice-Hall, 1963.

Becker, Russell J. *Family Pastoral Care.* Englewood Cliffs, N.J.: Prentice-Hall, 1965.

Bird, Joseph and Lois, *Marriage Is for Grownups: The Freedom of Sexual Love.* Garden City, N.Y.: Doubleday, 1967.

Blees, Robert A. *Counseling with Teen-Agers*. Englewood Cliffs, N.J.: Prentice-Hall, 1965.

Bowers, Margaretta K., et al. *Counseling the Dying*. New York: Nelson, 1964.

Bosco, Antoinette. *Marriage Encounter: The Rediscovery of Love*. St. Meinrad, Ind.: Abbey Press, 1972.

Brown, J. Paul. *Counseling with Senior Citizens*. Englewood Cliffs, N.J.: Prentice-Hall, 1964.

Bruder, Ernest E. *Ministering to Deeply Troubled People*. Englewood Cliffs, N.J.: Prentice-Hall, 1963.

Campanelle, T. C. *Counseling Parents of Mentally Retarded Children*. Englewood Cliffs, N.J.: Prentice-Hall, 1965.

Caplan, Ruth B., et al. *Helping the Helpers to Help: Mental Health Consultation to Aid Clergymen in Pastoral Work*. New York: Seabury Press, 1972.

Carkhuff, Robert R., and Bernard G. Berenson. *Beyond Counseling and Therapy*. New York: Holt, Rinehart and Winston, 1967.

Clinebell, Howard. *Crisis and Growth: Helping Your Troubled Child*. Philadelphia: Fortress Press, 1971.

Dechant, Emerald V. *How to Be Happily Married*. New York: Alba House, 1972.

Devlin, William Joseph. *Psychodynamics of Personality Development*. Staten Island, N.Y.: Alba House, 1965.

Evely, Louis. *Training Children for Maturity*, trans. by Edmund Bonin. Westminster, Md.: Newman Press, 1967.

Farnsworth, Dana L., and Francis J. Braceland, eds. *Psychiatry, the Clergy, and Pastoral Counseling*. Collegeville, Minn.: St. John's University Press, Institute for Mental Health, 1969.

Harris, Thomas Allen. *Counseling the Serviceman and His Family*. Englewood Cliffs, N.J.: Prentice-Hall, 1964.

Jackson, Edgar N. *When Someone Dies*. Philadelphia: Fortress Press, 1971.

Johnson, Paul E. *The Middle Years*. Philadelphia: Fortress Press, 1971.

Kandle, George C. *Ministering to Prisoners and Their Families*. Englewood Cliffs, N.J.: Prentice-Hall, 1968.

Kelleher, Stephen J. *Divorce and Remarriage for Catholics*. Garden City, N.Y.: Doubleday, 1973.

Kemp, Charles F. *Counseling with College Students*. Englewood Cliffs, N.J.: Prentice-Hall, 1964.

Kreis, Bernadine, and Alice Pattie. *Up from Grief*. Englewood Cliffs, N.J.: Prentice-Hall, 1965.

Mallett, Harold M. *Keeping Peace in the Family*. Nashville: Abingdon Press, 1973.

Pretzel, Paul W. *Understanding and Counseling the Suicidal Person*. Nashville: Abingdon Press, 1972.

Ryan, Mary Perkins. *Helping the Adolescents Grow Up in Christ*. New York: Paulist Press, 1966.

Salz, Victor. *Between Husband and Wife*. New York: Paulist Press, 1972.

Satir, Virginia. *Conjoint Family Therapy*, rev. ed. Palo Alto, Cal.: Science and Behavior Books, 1967.

Scherzer, Carl J. *Ministering to the Dying*. Englewood Cliffs, N.J.: Prentice-Hall, 1963.

Seifert, Harvey, and Howard J. Clinebell, Jr. *Personal Growth and Social Changes*. Philadelphia: Westminster Press, 1969.

Stewart, Charles William. *The Minister as Marriage Counselor*. Nashville: Abingdon Press, 1970.

Stone, Howard W. *Suicide and Grief*. Philadelphia: Fortress Press, 1972.

Terkelsen, Helen E. *Counseling the Unwed Mother*. Englewood Cliffs, N.J.: Prentice-Hall, 1964.

Weber, Carlo A. *Pastoral Psychology: New Trends and Practice*. New York: Sheed and Ward, 1970.

Wiese, Bennard R., and Uman G. Steinmetz. *Everything You Need to Know to Stay Married and Like It*. Grand Rapids, Mich.: Zondevan Publishing House, 1972.

Workshop in Psychological Counseling, Catholic University of America, *Psychological Counseling of Adolescents*, ed. by Raymond J. Steimel. Washington, D.C.: Catholic University of America Press, 1961.

III

PASTORAL COUNSELING AND SPIRITUAL AND MORAL VALUES

Bier, William C., ed. *Conscience: Freedoms and Limitations* (Proceedings of the Institute in Pastoral Psychology, 1969). New York: Fordham University Press, 1971.

Hulme, William E. *Am I Losing My Faith*. Philadelphia: Fortress Press, 1971.

May, Rollo. *Love and Will*. New York: Norton, 1969.

———. *Power and Innocence*. New York: Norton, 1972.

Nouwen, Henri J. *Creative Ministry*. Garden City, N.Y.: Doubleday, 1971.

———. *With Open Hands*. Notre Dame, Ind.: Ave Maria Press, 1972.

———. *The Wounded Healer: Ministry in Contemporary Society*. Garden City, N.Y.: Doubleday, 1972.

———. *Aging*. Garden City, N.Y.: Doubleday, 1974.

O'Doherty, Eamonn Feichin, and S. Desmond McGrath, eds. *The Priest and Mental Health*. Staten Island, N.Y.: Alba House, 1963.

Rahner, Karl. *Belief Today*. New York: Sheed and Ward, 1967.
———. *Grace in Freedom*, trans. by Hilda Graef. New York, Herder and Herder, 1969.
———. *Theological Investigations*, vol. II, trans. by David Bourke, London, Darton, Longman & Todd, 1974.
Tillich, Paul. *My Search for Absolutes*. New York: Simon and Schuster, 1967.
Williams, Daniel Day. *The Spirit and Forms of Love*. New York: Harper & Row, 1968.

REFERENCES FOR SPECIFIC COUNSELING TECHNIQUES

Behavioral Therapy
Eysenck, H. J., ed. *Behaviour Therapy and the Neuroses*. New York: Pergamon Press, 1960.
Wolpe, J. *Psychotherapy by Reciprocal Inhibition*. Stanford, Cal.: Stanford University Press, 1958.

Client-Centered Therapy
Rogers, C. R. *Counseling and Psychotherapy*. Boston: Houghton Mifflin, 1942.
———. *Client-Centered Therapy*. Boston: Houghton Mifflin, 1951.
———. *On Becoming a Person*. Boston: Houghton Mifflin, 1961.

Existential Therapy
Frankl, Viktor E. *Man's Search for Meaning: An Introduction to Logotherapy*. New York: Pocket Books, 1973.

Gestalt Therapy
Fagan, Joen, and Irma Lee Shepherd. *Life Techniques in Gestalt Therapy*. New York: Harper & Row, 1973.

Rational-Emotive Therapy
Ellis, Albert. *Growth Through Reason: Verbatim Cases in Rational-Emotive Therapy*. Palo Alto, Cal.: Science and Behavior Books, 1971.
———, and Robert A. Harper. *A Guide to Rational Living*. North Hollywood, Cal.: Wilshire Book Company, 1973.

Reality Therapy
Glasser, William. *Reality Therapy: A New Approach to Psychiatry*. New York: Harper & Row, 1965.

Transactional Analysis
Berne, Eric. *Games People Play*. New York: Grove Press, 1964.